ENDORSEMENTS FO

Eat simply so that others may simply eat. With Rice & Beans мол.., International showed us how the act of eating simply can connect us in love to vulnerable children thousands of miles away. *A Common Meal* draws us even deeper into that experience. It is informative, inspirational, and challenging, of course. And yet its recipes, tips, and group implementation guide make it extremely practical, too. It's just the kind of handbook my community needs to make the most out of Rice & Beans Month. *A Common Meal* is a gift to the Church. I'm so grateful to Lahash International for enfolding us into this important work.

— **John Pattison**, co-author of *Slow Church: Cultivating Community
in the Patient Way of Jesus*

Solidarity. A word often used but rarely practiced... sometimes because we don't know how. That's why I'm so grateful for *A Common Meal*. Filled with Christ-centered devotions, inspiring stories and diverse recipes, this helpful guide offers a practical and powerful way for individuals, families and churches to identify with our global brothers and sisters, and to be transformed in the process. I have been blown away over the years by the amazing work of Lahash International, and I know many in our church who have been impacted through participating in Rice & Beans Month.

— **Joshua Ryan Butler**, pastor of local & global outreach at Imago Dei
Community and author of *The Skeletons in God's Closet*

In his Rule for life together in community, St. Benedict noted three common practices that bind people together: praying, meeting, and eating. In a world of fast food and individualized diets, *A Common Meal* is more than a cookbook. It's more than a devotional. It's an invitation to recover one of the basic practices of beloved community.

— **Jonathan Wilson-Hartgrove**, author of *Strangers at My Door*

Lahash is challenging us not only by their words, but giving us a practical tool to stand in solidarity with those who experience life differently. *A Common Meal* is a welcome, creative, and spiritually-forming guide. Don't just read this book. Simplify your life, stand with the poor, share your resources, and be transformed in the process.

— **Leroy Barber**, global executive director of Word Made Flesh and
co-author of *Red, Brown, Yellow, Black, White—Who's More Precious
In God's Sight?: A call for diversity in Christian missions and ministry*

A Common Meal: A Devotional and Practical Guide to Rice & Beans Month
©2014 Lahash International

Published by Lahash International, Portland, Oregon
www.lahash.org

Permission to quote from the following sources is gratefully acknowledged:
"A Place at the Table" by Chris Seay
"Rich Christians in an Age of Hunger" by Ronald J. Sider

All written text, recipes, and photos, unless otherwise indicated, are submitted by Lahash International staff, volunteers, and child sponsors. All photographs used by permission.

Editorial Team:
Casey Schilperoort
Jen Johnson
Dan Holcomb
Interior Design & Layout:
Casey Schilperoort
Will Campbell
Matthew Mahder
Professional Photography:
Will Campbell
Nate Grubbs
Cover Design:
Vance Reeser

The internet addresses printed in this book are accurate at the time of publication, and provided as a resource. Lahash International does not guarantee their content or permanence.

A COMMON MEAL

A Devotional and Practical Guide
to Rice & Beans Month

LAHASH
GRASSROOTS PARTNERSHIP WITH AFRICA

CONTENTS

Your Introduction to

RICE & BEANS MONTH

THE GOOD, THE BAD, AND THE HUNGRY

Several years ago, I took an honest look at our organization, and this is what I saw: We were a team of young people with a relational, grassroots vision of ministry. We were pouring ourselves out on behalf of desperate people in East Africa. Our growing Child Sponsorship Program was making an impact in hundreds of lives. We were actively supporting incredibly dedicated East African leaders and their local ministries.

Although these were all good things, I observed a gnawing hunger creeping in. Our personal spiritual cores were running on empty. Team members, including me, were suffering from burnout and making big mistakes. We desperately needed change. We couldn't solve these issues on our own.

We turned to God for help. And we began to learn deeper lessons about Christian spiritual practices that would help to mature us in our faith and prompt us to daily savor the salvation and grace of Christ Jesus. It was during this time of spiritual renewal that we created a very unusual yearly event. Our core community committed to a month of eating more simply and donating the money we saved to buy food for families in East Africa. We called it "Rice & Beans Month."

Rice & Beans Month helped bring transformation to our spiritual life, and gave us another practical way to care for vulnerable kids. **They had a food crisis, we had a spiritual crisis. God used Rice & Beans Month to address both types of hunger.**

Rice & Beans Month quickly expanded far beyond our Portland-based ministry community to include participants all over the world. We've seen fundamental change in people's understanding of finances, generosity, God's provision, and their dependence on his sustenance. And as you will discover through many stories in this book, the impact in East Africa continues to grow as well. By God's grace, increasing numbers of people are seeking God together through this movement, and we are becoming more integrated and connected as the global Body of Christ.

So welcome to Rice & Beans Month! My prayer is that through this event you will be transformed more into the image of Christ as you savor his delicious grace and submit yourself in daily living sacrifice to him.

Dan Holcomb
Founder and Executive Director
of Lahash International

WHAT IS
RICE & BEANS MONTH?

Each year since 2010, Rice & Beans Month participants have spent the month of March (or the 40 days of Lent) putting love into action through three central themes:

1. **Simplicity:** altering our diets to emphasize basic and inexpensive meals
2. **Solidarity:** standing in unity with our brothers and sisters in East Africa who have limited resources and inadequate nutrition
3. **Sharing:** donating our saved money so that vulnerable kids and their families can receive much-needed nutritional support

The money donated by participants is used to improve food security for the children and families served by Lahash's partner organizations in East Africa. Some funds are designated for supplemental nutrition, some for projects that produce food in sustainable ways, and some for emergency food assistance in times of crisis.

By intentionally eating simple foods that mirror the diet of our East African friends, we spend far less than usual on groceries, and we connect our lives with theirs in meaningful ways. In doing so, we disconnect from some of the unhealthy patterns of western culture that can keep us physically full while leaving us spiritually empty. God faithfully uses Rice & Beans Month to satisfy both physical and spiritual hunger through the sharing of a common meal.

Let your love for God and others become as tangible
as a bowl of rice and beans.

To learn more, visit
EATRICEANDBEANS.COM

COMMON SYMPTOMS

Chronic hunger and malnutrition have many devastating effects on the body; here are just a few: *impaired vision, numbness in hands and feet, lack of endurance, stunted growth, decreased heart function, weakness, confusion and inability to focus.* Millions of people's bodies endure these ailments daily in East Africa. But consider this same list of symptoms from a spiritual rather than physical perspective. Just as physical hunger puts the body at risk, spiritual hunger takes its toll on the Body of Christ. The truth is that hunger weakens all of us. Whether in body or in spirit, we all need to be filled.

We are conditioned in western culture to pack our lives with work, activities, food, technology, entertainment … *stuff.* But material abundance cannot address our spiritual hunger. Our stuff can only give the illusion of fullness, obscuring the lingering sense that our deepest needs are still unmet.

God desires to satisfy both physical and spiritual hunger, and he is clear about what it will take for that to happen. In the first twelve verses of Isaiah 58, God tells his people (loosely paraphrased), *"You have expected me to be impressed with your spiritual practices and to act on your behalf, but your rituals are empty. Your brothers and sisters are in need, and you are not working to alleviate their suffering. Your darkened spiritual condition is directly tied to their physical condition. But your healing will come as you seek their healing. When you truly share my heart for the vulnerable among you, then the lives of all my beloved children will be restored, and all their hunger filled."*

Friends, let's partner with God to address this list of common symptoms with sincerity, humility, and love. Our commitment to care for the vulnerable will positively impact the physical health of many suffering people. And as we deepen our spiritual sensitivity, the Body of Christ will be strengthened as well. This creative, communal event is an opportunity to experience the ways that God can satisfy both physical and spiritual hunger through a simple shared meal.

We joyfully invite you to join us in this endeavor.

OPENING OUR EYES

In a dusty Tanzanian town, a boy named Eliya lives in a small house with a large extended family. Several years ago, although the house languished in a state of over-crowding and disrepair, its residents warmly welcomed Lahash founder Dan Holcomb and a local pastor, Manase Mhana.

At the time of their visit, Eliya had recently been accepted into the Child Sponsorship Program. Dan and Manase wanted to get a better sense of the specific issues he faced. (If you'd like to see their visit with Eliya, watch the video called "Dan & Eliya" at *eatriceandbeans.com/video*.) Here is Dan's account of their time there:

> *Eliya's family consisted of three adult relatives and approximately 25 siblings and cousins living in three rooms. Many of them were HIV-positive, including Eliya. His mother was HIV-positive and had passed away, leaving Eliya to grow up without her as he struggled with the same disease.*
>
> *For dinner on the night of our visit, Eliya's aunt served a corn paste called "ugali" with a small bowl of cooked greens. It was barely enough for me, Manase, Eliya, and two of the adult relatives to share. The five of us ate together, squeezed into one of the small rooms.*
>
> *After finishing the food, Manase and I stepped out into the hallway and antici-pated seeing the rest of the family enjoying the same meal. We were overwhelmed to discover that the family had served us the only food in the home. The rest of the children were to go hungry that night. Manase and I purchased some bread and tea for the kids so they would have something to eat before they went to bed.*

Dan and Manase spent the night in Eliya's home, sharing a mattress and mosquito net, with Eliya crammed next to them. Seeing firsthand that Eliya and the other children in the home lacked consistent access to food was a hard reality for Dan and Manase to accept. In the morning, they ate a modest break-fast of porridge with the family before continuing to the local church that hosts the Lahash Sponsorship Program. Sponsorship gave Eliya access to education, healthcare, anti-retroviral drugs, discipleship in the gospel, and much more. Yet it was not enough to ensure that his entire family had sufficient food each day.

Eliya and many other children like him are the inspiration that fuels our com-mitment to Rice & Beans Month. Participating is one small step toward following in the ways of Jesus and inviting meaningful outcomes for families like Eliya's and for ourselves. We eagerly anticipate seeing increased compassion and action that helps to alleviate the suffering of vulnerable people. We trust that we will see our entire global community growing more and more into the image of Christ.

Throughout the Bible, God clearly tells us that our love for God is demonstrated in the way we treat vulnerable humans around us. Jesus Christ gives this message in the gospels, and the book of I John is especially clear that the way we love our brothers and sisters reveals the honesty of our love for God. We cannot separate love of God from love of neighbor. (*See specifically I John 3:16–24, and 4:13–21.*)

However, the problems of poverty in the developing world, and even in our own communities, can feel far away and unrelated to our lives. Many of us live in a fairly protected environment and have little or no contact with suffering people.

Very few of us have the opportunity to travel to East Africa and stay overnight in the home of a child like Eliya. And yet, all of us can intentionally focus on the wider world around us. As we do so, we quickly come face-to-face with the homeless, the hungry, the immigrants, the outcasts, and the sick. Rice & Beans Month not only increases our awareness of suffering people and their needs, but also guides us in taking steps toward positive change.

It's not as difficult as you might think. We hope you will see in another family's story that starting out small may be the best way to ensure you continue.

A SMALL BEGINNING

Jen Johnson, a writer and editor with Lahash, shares her family's story of participating in Rice & Beans Month.

This photo was taken not long after my family participated in the first Rice & Beans Month in 2010. Our kids were young! We were not yet very involved with Lahash, but because my husband, Keith, and I had spent time in East Africa early in our marriage, we were excited for an opportunity to reconnect with that part of the world.

The concept of Rice & Beans Month was great. The biggest obstacle? Coming up with a realistic plan for ourselves to actually eat rice and beans.

Honestly, we were a little intimidated by the whole idea. Our youngest child wouldn't stay in her seat at dinner even when her *favorite* foods were offered. Serving up rice and beans seemed like a guarantee of tears and tantrums around the table, parents included. We had a strong tug in our hearts urging us to participate, but this was competing with the strong wills of a four- and five-year-old. So here is what we did:

We ate one dinner of rice and beans per week. That's right, a whopping total of four meals of rice and beans over the course of 31 days. In that season of life, it was just the right amount.

Our goal was to make Rice & Beans Month an annual event for our family. We figured that causing our children to hate it the very first time would be detrimental to that goal. We explained the month to them at a level they could understand, and we focused a lot more on the concepts and purpose than on the food itself. I was amazed at how quickly their eyes and hearts opened to vulnerable children half a world away. However, even with the obvious positive impact of the month right before us, Keith and I had a hard time shaking the feeling that we "weren't doing it right" or that our family's way of participating was falling short of a much higher standard.

So even though no specific rules have ever been laid out for Rice & Beans Month, I've had questions concerning what we are and are not "allowed" to eat, ever since the first year. And I know I'm not alone. Here's the real deal: the **theme is rice and beans.** It offers a good protein source, it's inexpensive and easily accessible, and it represents the staple foods of East Africa well. **This theme is open to interpretation by every participant.** There are no frequency requirements, no rigid meal plans, and no Rice & Beans Police to interrogate you about your grocery receipts and food choices.

We encourage you to simply pray about how best to participate, and then follow God's leading. **Please don't miss an opportunity to interact with God about this experience because you're too concerned with non-existent rules.** Discuss it with your family, community group, church, or whoever is joining you. Consider, first and foremost, that all of us are being invited by God to partner in the building of his kingdom on earth. There is no right or wrong way to do that when our hearts are aligned with his. Embark on this journey in faith, and trust that your approach is perfect for you.

For my family's first year, it was all about taking small steps, and the same was true for Lahash. Dan and Manase witnessed a heartbreaking level of poverty on that first visit with Eliya. But then the donations from the first Rice & Beans Month were used to purchase bulk quantities of maize flour and beans for Eliya's family and many others! Seeing the video about the day when all of that food was distributed erased any hesitation we still felt about engaging in this event as a family. (You can see the video from that first year, too! It's called "Welcome to Rice & Beans Month" at *eatriceandbeans.com/video*.) We knew that providing supplemental food items was not a long-term answer to their hunger issues, but it greatly encouraged us to see the help that was made possible even through small efforts like ours.

THE ROUGH PATCH

You might assume that such a positive impact on our family and on families in East Africa fully fueled our joyful and whole-hearted participation in subsequent years. And you would be wrong in that assumption.

I did learn (the hard way) that starting Rice & Beans Month in March goes much better if you do a little bit of preparation in February. So one year we got all organized and had a few brainstorming sessions a couple weeks in advance. We discussed which rice and beans meals we liked the best and what we were going to eat for breakfasts. We talked about the kids in East Africa and how much it would help them. I thought we were making some real progress until one daughter began to express repeatedly, "I don't want to eat that. I *don't* want to *eat that.*" Did I mention it was only February?

Rice & Beans Month is a challenge. It truly is. A challenge with huge potential to change your life and the lives of many suffering people. But that's not always the focus when you try a new recipe and it turns out yucky and your children begin to cry and then you join them and you all go to bed experiencing true solidarity with the hungry for reasons you can't fully articulate in that moment. (At least, I've heard of that type of thing happening to … some people.)

And then, somehow, you start to hear the voice of the Spirit over the growling in your stomach. God surprises you. Fills you. And lets you see for yourself why it's worth it.

One glimpse of that came during what I would call a "Rice & Beans Rough Patch." Our girls each came home from school reporting that they had been offered candy. We assumed at first that they had eaten it, based on their utter lack of enthusiasm for anything related to rice and beans. We were surprised to hear that both of them had turned it down. As our youngest was telling her story to Keith, it was clear that she had responded to the gentle voice of God's Spirit. She got teary-eyed as she relived the moment and said, "I sacrificed it, Daddy."

That was the end of our rough patch that year, and a welcome turning point. Seeing the hearts of our children responding to the heart of God gave us spiritual incentive to persevere. We knew from the beginning that Rice & Beans Month would influence hungry families for good, and we were humbled to realize that our family was one of them.

SEEING THE IMPACT

Each year, our family has ventured deeper spiritually, increased our meals of rice and beans, and shared more money with our friends in East Africa. And it seems like many other families would say the same, because the donations multiplied enough to start and sustain a special feeding program for HIV-positive children at one of the Lahash partnerships.

Before Rice & Beans Month, I knew nothing about the nutritional needs of HIV-positive kids. It was sobering to find out that the World Health Organization recommends HIV-infected children consume at least 10% more calories than non-infected children. When an HIV-positive child is fighting an illness (which is very common), the recommendation is for a calorie increase of 20–30% or even more! And even with a well-balanced diet and drug therapies, kids with HIV are far more likely to have stunted growth and slow weight gain than healthy kids. Knowing that the diets of kids like Eliya usually lacked *basic* nutrition made *extra* nutrition seem nearly impossible. Thankfully, Rice & Beans funds made a big difference.

If you go to *eatriceandbeans.com/video* and click on "A Special Nutrition Program," you'll see our friend Eliya, looking much taller and stronger than he did in the video of Dan's visit! Eliya and another young boy named Gabriel are mentioned specifically because their health was of such great concern. The two boys resorted to picking through trash piles to try to find food. Now, Eliya and twenty-plus other HIV-positive children receive four supplemental meals per week of rice, beans, meat, greens, and fruit. That is a huge increase for kids who were not eating every day. This added nutrition has most likely saved Eliya's life.

The program has also provided a place for these vulnerable kids to form friendships with each other and with the staff. They are loved and discipled. They play and sing. They make art projects. They are able to take their medications more consistently and sleep more restfully because their bellies are full of nutritious food.

I was amazed to realize that changing our diets for one month could help to change the diets of these children for an entire year.

LOOKING FORWARD TO MORE

During the fifth year of Rice & Beans Month, our kids engaged at a level I never could have imagined during "the crying years." They wrote a skit with Keith and me that we performed at a kick-off dinner hosted by Lahash. They rallied extended family members to join us for the month. They brought print materials to school to show their teachers and classmates, inviting them to participate even if it was just for one meal. One Sunday, we picked them up from their class at church, and the head of the children's ministry complimented us on the great speech they gave to all the 2nd- through 5th-graders about Rice & Beans Month. We had no idea they were planning to do that!

We got into a good groove with meals at home as well. We stuck with whole grain hot cereals for breakfast, and lunches of bean stews, hearty lentil salads, or leftovers. Snacks of fruits, veggies, and nuts were helpful, as was maintaining a rotation of our favorite rice and beans recipes for dinner. However, even with some strategic breaks, those favorite recipes felt monotonous at times. In those moments, our kids were often the ones to point out the prominently-displayed photos of our precious sponsored children, Anjelina and Baraka. We regularly pray for them to have good healthy food, so it helped to remember that we were eating rice and beans specifically to bring that about. Keith and I saw so much growth in the girls' self-discipline, generosity, and perseverance. We were inspired by their example.

Dan asked me afterward if we thought we would continue to participate in Rice & Beans Month in coming years, or if we felt ready to move on to something else. After thinking for a minute, I realized I couldn't come up with a reason to stop. Rough patches and all, it has become a treasured part of our family's year. And such great strides are being made in securing food for vulnerable people we love.

For example, in Eliya's community, the Tanzanian church members saw the impact of Rice & Beans Month on the local people. The church members, many living in poverty themselves, joined the effort and streamlined their already-simple meals. Then they took up a collection in church, offering money, bags of beans, and sacks of rice. The commitment of western Christians on the other side of the world moved the Tanzanian church to greater generosity!

The news of their effort made it to the office of the Prime Minister of Tanzania. In turn, he donated a goat, rice, beans, sugar, and oil for a celebration dinner for 175 of the community's poorest and most vulnerable families. Local program director, Tiffanee Wright, commented, "Campaigns like these help us get a glimpse of the beauty of the Kingdom of Heaven." Why wouldn't we want to be a part of that?

Our little family in Portland, Oregon, may not have gained the attention of any high-ranking government officials, but we have moved from "Why are we doing this?" and "I don't want to eat that" all the way to "Why would we stop doing this? It's completely worth it." That is growth, my friends, and we look forward to more.

READY TO BE FILLED

What will all of this mean for Eliya? It gives him the chance to live a long and healthy life. He might complete school, pursue meaningful work, and follow Jesus as he follows his dreams. He might live to see his entire town free from the devastating impact of chronic hunger and malnutrition. None of that would be possible if he was still picking food out of trash piles. Eventually his health would decline too far, and HIV/AIDS would steal another life too early.

As we begin Rice & Beans Month, let's anticipate that God will nourish our souls to the same extent that wholesome food and compassionate care are nourishing Eliya. There are many options for how to participate, and all of them invite God to meet our inner hunger for deep spiritual satisfaction. Let the promise of such rich results encourage us through these coming weeks of choosing to eat in solidarity with the poor.

Deciding to join this adventure is the first step to getting involved, but then you must figure out what to do! Continue reading to explore the practical side of Rice & Beans Month.

HOW TO USE THIS BOOK

A *Common Meal* is designed to help individuals, families, and entire churches engage in Rice & Beans Month in unique and meaningful ways. You'll find no requirement that you adhere to a set of rules or regulations; we've noticed that when God stirs people's hearts to participate, he also guides them in figuring out *how*. This book can help in that process whether you savor every page or sample tidbits here and there. There are four main sections to enrich your experience:

- **"How To" section** – Hey, you're reading it right now! With all the basic guidelines and big themes, this section alone can equip new participants to begin their first Rice & Beans Month.

- **Devotions** – Here, you will find daily meditations for days 1-31, and nine extra days of material for those adapting Rice & Beans Month as a 40-day Lenten experience. Each day includes a scripture, a devotional, a section for kids, and a prayer. *(pages 25–107)*

- **Stories** – Rice & Beans Month is changing lives! We've included a variety of short articles that offer personal experiences, examples of the impact in East Africa, and lots of encouragement for the journey. *(pages 109–149)*

- **Recipes** – The benefits of several years' worth of food experiences are yours, plus the tried-and-true cooking advice of a wide variety of participants. *(pages 151–182)*

- ***Bonus!*** – There are a few useful "tip sheets" at the end: *Tips for Everyone, Tips for Families with Kids*, and a *Guide for Groups or Churches*. *(pages 185–191)* These items are also available for download at *eatriceandbeans.com*.

SHARING AN UNCOMMON MEAL

Many of us are accustomed to a wide range of food choices. We can enjoy eating in restaurants that serve countless types of food, we shop at a variety of stores (even if only to get the best deals), and perhaps we are able grow some of our own food or source it locally from various farms. During Rice & Beans Month, we deviate significantly from our typical eating patterns, and make choices that are decidedly *un*common within western society. **Intentionally eliminating most of our food options is both cross-cultural and counter-cultural.** This "uncommon meal" is a challenge with the rare capacity to feed our bodies while nourishing our longing for something beyond the western status quo.

As we embrace food staples from other cultures while directly contradicting the norms of our own culture, let's keep our focus on three central themes:

Simplicity
We choose foods that are *commonly accessible* all over the world. Ordinary staple foods form the basic foundation of nutritious meals. We purposefully eliminate a lot of the diversity and excess in our usual food choices.

Solidarity
Our meals more closely mirror the type of diet available in most of East Africa. It's one thing to know how they eat every day; it's another thing to eat in a similar way ourselves. We connect with our East African brothers and sisters by having a daily experience *in common* with them.

Sharing
We want balanced nutrition to be as consistent, frequent, and *common* for our East African family as it is for us. This will require generous sharing on our part! We will share life, food, prayers, and spiritual connection this month, and we will also donate our saved money to purchase supplemental food items and fund sustainable food projects.

Together, we're making an uncommon choice to share a common meal.

For a great video summary of the month, check out
"Rice & Beans Month Basics" at *eatriceandbeans.com/video.*

SO ... WHAT DO WE EAT?

For the poorest people on our planet, meals (when available) are predictable and simple. They are based on staples of rice, corn, wheat, potatoes, and beans/legumes in some form or another. These common meals are repeated day after day, offering a decent balance of protein and carbohydrates. They cost less and are more easily accessible than meat or other animal products.

Rice and beans are readily available across East Africa. (And even more common than rice are forms of maize not grown in North America.) Although the exact preparation varies from region to region, some combination of these simple ingredients can be found in many homes.

As you figure out how to make simplicity and solidarity a part of your unique approach to Rice & Beans Month, here are some general guidelines to consider:

Getting Ready

Many previous participants have learned the hard way that Day One is really tough if you haven't made at least a couple of preparations. Here are the two most important things to do in January and February that will help you begin well:

- **Pray about it.** Keep Rice & Beans Month in your spiritual and practical field of vision. *"God, what are you inviting us to?" "What goals will help us grow this year?"*
- **Buy some rice and beans.** You will want to wake up on the first day with these items already in your pantry, perhaps even cooked and ready to eat.

Those are the big things. For more ideas, check out the "tip sheets" toward the back of the book on pages 152 and 187–189 (or posted online at *eatriceandbeans.com*).

Food Choices

The heart of this event is not about specific menu plans, and yet we still must make decisions, set goals, and buy groceries. Here are some possible answers to the question, "What do we eat?"

- Choose to skip the "extras" like coffee drinks, sodas, fast food, and convenience foods. As a way to stand in solidarity, emphasize simple meals made mostly from scratch.
- If rice and beans seems unrealistic for three meals a day, consider other ways to simplify your options for breakfast and/or lunch. For example, emphasize simple grains like oatmeal rather than boxed breakfast cereals.

- Consider eliminating meat, dairy, bread, sweets and desserts, and processed foods from your diet. These are things our East African friends very rarely eat, and are often the most expensive items on our grocery lists.
- Make rice and beans dishes the main focus of your meals, prepared with a variety of spices, seasonings, condiments, and veggies.
- Emphasize fruits, veggies, and nuts for sides and snacks, rather than processed snack foods. Perhaps consider eliminating snacks altogether.

Common Modifications

While there are families and groups who choose to focus all their meals on rice and beans, there have also been many people who have embraced the spirit and intention of this event while modifying food choices in creative ways:

- Some incorporate a "celebration meal" or a "celebration day" periodically to take a break from rice and beans. (Those participating for Lent have Sundays as celebration days.)
- Some stick with fairly normal breakfasts and lunches, and emphasize rice and beans for the evening meal only.
- Some, due to allergies or food-sensitivity issues, have adapted other low-cost staple food options instead of rice or beans.
- Most participants include additional legumes like lentils and additional low-cost grain options like barley or corn meal.

Any of these options fit well within the scope of Rice & Beans Month. Perhaps we could rename it something like "Inexpensively-Obtained Variety of Grains Combined with Assorted Beans, Legumes, and Miscellaneous Fresh Produce Month," but it just doesn't roll off the tongue quite as easily.

So be assured that while there are important reasons behind the emphasis on the specific foods of rice and beans, **the spirit and intention are far more important**. If you have special considerations, or would simply like to ease into the whole idea, please do! Tailor your approach so that the dietary changes are challenging, yet sustainable for the duration of the event.

As the apostle Paul points out at the beginning of I Corinthians 13, we can do all sorts of radical things to benefit ourselves and others, but without love, we gain nothing. **Let love be your motivation on this journey**. If your love for God and others has expanded by the end of Rice & Beans Month, that is a far better measure of success than how many meals of rice and beans you ate.

HOW WILL YOU GET INVOLVED?

Join a community of people who are stripping away the excesses in their diets as an act of solidarity with our friends in East Africa. The money we save and donate will go directly toward increasing nutrition and food security for vulnerable kids and families. Here are several ways to get involved with Rice & Beans Month:

- **Allow God to shape your heart.** Use the devotions in *A Common Meal* to focus your prayers and connect with God during the month.

- **Engage online.** Watch a few videos at *eatriceandbeans.com/video* that offer glimpses into the lives of the children who helped inspire this event. Visit *Facebook.com/EatRiceAndBeans* or *eatriceandbeans.com* to connect with others for spiritual and practical inspiration. You can even share some of your own recipes, stories, or photos.

- **Let us know you're participating!** Visit *eatriceandbeans.com*, enter your name and email address, and click "I'm in!" to let us know you're eating simple meals of rice and beans during March (or Lent). Whether it's for three meals a day or three meals during the month, we'll be excited to know that you have officially joined us.

- **Support each other.** As any previous participant would agree, this event is greatly enhanced by the presence of family, friends, or church members alongside you. Share meals, recipes, and encouragement throughout the month.

- **Host a Rice & Beans potluck.** Whether as a "pre-event kickoff" in February or a morale-builder in March, invite your friends and family to a communal rice and beans meal. Share the reasons you are participating as you invite your community to join you.

- **Prepare to give.** Keep track of your food expenses during March/Lent, and subtract that total from a typical month's food spending. Any amount saved, whether from a single meal or an entire month of meals, will help put food on the plate of someone who truly needs it.

For more stories, videos, recipes, and updates, visit us online at

EatRiceAndBeans.com

DEVOTIONS

DAY 01

For this reason, ever since I heard about your faith in the Lord Jesus and your love for all God's people, I have not stopped giving thanks for you, remembering you in my prayers. I keep asking that the God of our Lord Jesus Christ, the glorious Father, may give you the Spirit of wisdom and revelation, so that you may know him better.

Ephesians 1:15–17

Friends, welcome to Rice & Beans Month. We are excited that you are joining us to explore a unique intersection of faith and food.

In today's scripture, Paul commends the faith of the church of Ephesus and their love for all the saints. Just as Paul is filled with gratitude to God for the Ephesians, we are grateful for YOU. We rejoice at the faith required to deny personal pleasures. We anticipate God's good work in your life, and we pray you grow in compassionate love toward others.

I want to say this clearly and with conviction: Expect your faith in Jesus and your love for the most vulnerable members of the global church to grow during this experience. As this happens, you will also be deeply challenged. Many of us are not accustomed to setting aside our normal eating patterns and natural desires for this length of time. We are choosing to offer our bodies as a daily sacrifice (Romans 12:1), and submit our patterns and desires to God in an unfamiliar way.

Paul's gratitude for the faith and love of the Ephesians prompts him to pray for them. He wants their spiritual senses to be sharper, that they might know God even better. It is through the power of God that our spiritual eyes are opened to his lavish and undeserved love. That love empowers us to do the good works that God has prepared in advance for us (Ephesians 2:10).

As you seek to submit your mind, body, soul, and strength to God in order to love him and love others, I want to pray Paul's prayer for you and ask you to join me in praying it over all the participants: *Lord, may our spiritual eyes be opened. May your Spirit give us new wisdom. May new maturity develop as we engage in the simple and earthy task of eating rice and beans.*

Amen.

Dan Holcomb, Executive Director of Lahash
Portland, Oregon

FOR KIDS

We're so glad you're participating in Rice & Beans Month that we made a video to welcome you! It's called "Welcome to Rice & Beans Month" and you can find it at *eatriceandbeans.com/video*.

Your family has chosen to eat rice and beans as a way to experience a simpler life, like our friends in East Africa. Since rice and beans are less expensive than our regular food, we'll get to share the money we save with hungry families in East Africa so that they can eat healthy, nutritious meals. What can you do to help? You can eat rice and beans, too! Eating rice and beans with a thankful attitude can be a big encouragement to your whole family. It is also a way to help you get to know God better, and to share the love he puts in your heart! For today, make a sign with your family that says you are eating rice and beans, hold it up, take a photo, and send the photo to Lahash at *info@eatriceandbeans.com*! It will remind us to keep you in our prayers, and our friends in East Africa would love to see it, too.

PRAYER

Loving God, as we begin today to change what we feed our bodies, we trust you to feed our hearts. Expose thoughts, attitudes, and beliefs that hinder the process of becoming more like Jesus. Transform us, guide us, encourage us, challenge us. Decrease the focus we place on ourselves and our own desires. Increase in us a heart of compassion for our brothers and sisters around the world who are struggling to secure their next meal. We begin this journey in humility and faith, seeking to know you better. Amen.

When the disciples reached the other side, they had forgotten to bring any bread. Jesus said to them, "Watch and beware of the leaven of the Pharisees and Sadducees." And they began discussing it among themselves, saying, "We brought no bread." But Jesus, aware of this, said, "O you of little faith, why are you discussing among yourselves the fact that you have no bread? Do you not yet perceive? Do you not remember the five loaves for the five thousand, and how many baskets you gathered? Or the seven loaves for the four thousand, and how many baskets you gathered? How is it that you fail to understand that I did not speak about bread? Beware of the leaven of the Pharisees and Sadducees." Then they understood that he did not tell them to beware of the leaven of bread, but of the teaching of the Pharisees and Sadducees.

Matthew 16:5–12 (ESV)

All of us can agree that food is pretty central to the experience of Rice & Beans Month, and to life in general. For me, that is both the blessing and challenge. I have to eat; I can't escape it. Once, twice, or even three times a day, my life is changed when I choose to eat in solidarity with the vulnerable. My life looks different. I miss bread. And like the disciples, I can get stuck there.

In today's scripture, the disciples are concerned about their food and just can't get past it. They even miss a lesson from their Teacher because they are convinced that Jesus is talking about the bread, too. You can almost hear Jesus trying to cut through their obsession with what they are (or are not) going to eat.

Jesus is using their physical circumstances to try to teach them something deeper. He is ready to do the same with Rice & Beans Month, to use this tangible change in diet to shape our hearts.

In Jesus' day, religious leaders wanted to make life about following their set of rules, right down to what one could and could not eat, and when. The end goal was to do it all correctly and reap the deserved rewards.

That same mentality can easily find its way into Rice & Beans Month. The most common questions I am asked are, "So what can you really eat? Only beans and rice? What about vegetables or a banana? Is it okay to have crackers if they are made with rice flour? I love cheese. What about cheese?" Even after years of participating, I still wrestle with similar questions. *Should I feel guilty about scooping my beans and rice with tortilla chips?* And there I am standing with the disciples, missing the point, asking Jesus about the bread … again.

My stomach and my heart can grumble loudly at times, making it difficult to hear anything else. Preoccupied with "bread," I risk missing the lessons Jesus has for me. Maybe you will find yourself in that same spot. But thankfully, we are not alone there.

Jesus reminds us that he is the Lord of abundance. He can feed a crowd of thousands or a handful of forgetful followers. He reminds us that this experience is all about our hearts and his kingdom. It's about listening for his voice above the grumbling sounds of our stomachs. As our meals unite us with the poor and hungry this month, our Teacher has much to tell us. Let's listen for his voice.

Casey Schilperoort, Media Director at Lahash
Portland, Oregon

FOR KIDS

Steven's teacher asked everyone in the class to sit in a circle for storytime. Steven knew all the rules, and he sat very still in his spot. He couldn't help looking all around the circle at his classmates, and he could hardly stand what he saw! Some of them were playing with their shoelaces, some were wiggling, and one kid was even blowing bubbles with his spit. Steven's friend, Lisa, was the worst. He couldn't believe how squirmy she was, stretching like she was in an exercise class or something!

When the story was over, the teacher started asking questions about it. Hands were going up all around the circle, but not Steven's. His cheeks turned red with embarrassment as he realized that he had been so busy worrying about what all of his friends were doing that he hadn't listened to the story at all. Lisa raised her hand for lots of the questions. Steven didn't know a single answer.

Steven did a great job of following the classroom rules, but all the other kids actually heard the story. If you could give Steven some advice, what would you say? Just like Steven and the disciples in the Bible story for today, we can be distracted by things that are actually not what's most important. That will be a big thing to remember during the entire time that we're eating rice and beans.

As a family, pray that God will help you stay focused on the most important things he wants to show you and teach you this month. Remember, there are lots of different ways to do Rice & Beans Month, and all of them are the right way!

PRAYER

Gracious God, we want to hear your voice. As we set aside unnecessary foods, help us also to set aside the distractions that prevent our hearts from connecting with yours. Encourage and challenge us, Holy Spirit, as only you can. Help us release anything that is not worth holding onto, so that we can fully cling to you and respond to your work within us. Amen.

Then the righteous will answer him, 'Lord, when did we see you hungry and feed you, or thirsty and give you something to drink? When did we see you a stranger and invite you in, or needing clothes and clothe you? When did we see you sick or in prison and go to visit you?' The King will reply, 'Truly I tell you, whatever you did for one of the least of these brothers and sisters of mine, you did for me.'

Matthew 25:37–40

It's amazing and humbling to realize that our Lord identifies with those in need, the "least of these." In fact, he calls them his brothers and sisters. But God is also interested in *our* hearts for the vulnerable. God cares where our time, money, and resources go because these choices reveal the motives of our hearts. He desires to see his love being made perfect in us through his Son, Jesus. What greater way to do that than by putting the needs of others before our own?

I've found that Rice & Beans Month really softens my heart to the daily choices I make and how those choices affect the vulnerable. It has given me a chance to become more aware of God's voice. God has spoken volumes into unbalanced areas of my life that had somehow become normal because of the culture in which I live and because of my own sin.

This whole experience could easily become focused on whether we indulge our food cravings or stick to the goals we've set for the month. I pray that we can move past that and discover a real desire to complete this journey in a way that brings us closer to God and increases our love of others. Hopefully, our food cravings will subside as we develop a stronger craving for God's Kingdom here on earth.

Simply by participating in Rice & Beans Month, you are standing united with your brothers and sisters in need, and you're sharing food with the hungry. I pray you are as encouraged by this as I am.

Katie Nelson, Sponsorship Director at Lahash
Portland, Oregon

FOR KIDS

In these verses, Jesus explains that when we feed people who are hungry or visit people who are lonely, it's like we're feeding Jesus and visiting Jesus! Every day that you eat rice and beans lets you provide food for people who are hungry, which is like making dinner for Jesus.

Go to *eatriceandbeans.com/video*, and watch the video called "More Than A Meal." You will see a whole bunch of the people that Jesus is talking about in this verse. Watch carefully, and you'll see the light of Jesus shining brightly in them!

PRAYER

We live to proclaim your name, Jesus! As you inspire us to action, may every good work bear fruit to feed a hungry world with your abundant love. Reveal your light in every face we see, until the light of your kingdom fills our vision. In every daily task and choice, help us to joyfully take hold of the life that is truly life. Amen.

Our desire is not that others might be relieved while you are hard pressed, but that there might be equality. At the present time your plenty will supply what they need, so that in turn their plenty will supply what you need. The goal is equality, as it is written: "The one who gathered much did not have too much, and the one who gathered little did not have too little."

II Corinthians 8:13–15

In today's scripture, Paul writes to a thriving urban church on behalf of hungry Christians in Jerusalem. The Corinthians have the financial means to send aid to needy sisters and brothers, but Paul makes it clear that there is more to it than simply a one-way request for *those who have* to provide for *those who have not.*

The idea that "your plenty will supply what they need" makes sense, but then Paul adds a puzzling phrase, "so that in turn their plenty will supply what you need." Will the Corinthians be suffering someday, and be glad for gifts from Jerusalem? Perhaps. But the more crucial point seems to be that Paul wanted the Corinthians to understand sharing as a two-way blessing.

It is important to give freely without expecting anything back, yet it is rare that giving flows only one direction in God's Kingdom. Our gifts may not be returned in like form, but the value of what is received may well be greater than our gift!

Our friends in East Africa are always incredibly welcoming of visitors from the U.S., and I have felt on each of my visits that the blessing of being with them was far greater repayment than the value of any gifts I might offer. One year, plans for a trip to Tanzania with my friend, Dave, came to a screeching halt when I was diagnosed with shingles. Of course I was disappointed that Dave and I would miss the adventure. But then as the days passed, the reality settled in that I would be deprived of the blessing that comes from being influenced by the faith and joy of African Christians. The pain of that realization surpassed the pain of the shingles. I knew my physical health was causing me to miss out on an immeasurable benefit to my spiritual health. Surely their plenty would have supplied my need and would have been a fair balance indeed.

May we move beyond any self-righteousness that comes through the false assumption that we are the only ones who have something to give. May our questionable sense that we are handing out the blessings be replaced by the deeper realization of equality in giving: each supplying the other's need out of their own abundance. May we lose our one-way concept of sharing and open our eyes to the two-way blessings of the Kingdom of God.

Jim Anderson, Lahash volunteer and child sponsor
Portland, Oregon

FOR KIDS

M any times when we think about the people around the world who are poor, all we think about are the things that we have and they don't. Although it is important for us to realize that many people don't have enough food or clean water or medicine, it is just as important to remember that they have many things we lack.

Sam is an old man who lives in Tanzania. He has leprosy, a disease that caused him to lose his fingers and toes. He lives at a hospital because he needs a lot of help to do everyday tasks like washing and feeding himself. Leisha, who works with Lahash in East Africa, got to know Sam when she first moved to Tanzania. "Although I tried to give him some things like bread and fruit from time to time, what Sam gave me was worth so much more. When I moved here and didn't know anyone, he was my first friend," she says. "His friendly smile and kind words have been so much more important to me than the bananas I have given to him."

Ask your parents to help you watch the video "Dan and Eliya" and pay attention not only to the things Eliya does not have, but to what you can learn from him that might help you in your life! You can find the video at *eatriceandbeans.com/video.*

PRAYER

H oly God, we confess that we have conformed to the patterns of this world. In doing so, we have selfishly disregarded the needs of others and fallen away from you. We offer ourselves to you today. Forgive us by your grace, transform us with your truth, and strengthen us with compassion that we might bear the burdens of our brothers and sisters. In gratitude for your countless gifts, may we seek to embody your generous love. Amen.

"For day after day they seek me out; they seem eager to know my ways, as if they were a nation that does what is right and has not forsaken the commands of its God. They ask me for just decisions and seem eager for God to come near them.

'Why have we fasted,' they say, 'and you have not seen it? Why have we humbled ourselves, and you have not noticed?'

"Yet on the day of your fasting, you do as you please and exploit all your workers. Your fasting ends in quarreling and strife, and in striking each other with wicked fists. You cannot fast as you do today and expect your voice to be heard on high.

"Is this the kind of fast I have chosen, only a day for people to humble themselves? Is it only for bowing one's head like a reed and for lying in sackcloth and ashes? Is that what you call a fast, a day acceptable to the LORD?

"Is not this the kind of fasting I have chosen: to loose the chains of injustice and untie the cords of the yoke, to set the oppressed free and break every yoke? Is it not to share your food with the hungry and to provide the poor wanderer with shelter– when you see the naked, to clothe them, and not to turn away from your own flesh and blood?"

Isaiah 58:2–7

These words in Isaiah are breathtaking. God is critiquing his people for pretentious and dishonest fasting. The people in Isaiah's day were expecting that their fasting would earn God's attention and favor. But their fasting was corrupted by their abuse of laborers, lack of humility, arguments, fights, and injustice. God makes it clear that this is not what he desires.

These words in Isaiah speak just as strongly to our spiritual lives today. Too often our spiritual practices are for show and only serve to hide dishonesty, injustice, and rebellion. God is looking for fresh and pure intentions and actions. Instead of congratulating ourselves for choosing this fast, let us allow the lack of comfort foods, convenience, and variety to sharpen our spiritual awareness.

How do our regular food choices affect workers in our communities or around the world? In what ways do we engage in superficial spirituality while walking past poor, naked, and hungry neighbors? Does our lifestyle contribute to the suffering of others? Ask God's Spirit to bring conviction to all areas of our lives. May this fast increase our hunger to see the oppressed set free and to see God's Kingdom come!

Dan Holcomb, Executive Director of Lahash
Portland, Oregon

FOR KIDS

Fasting is a strange thing. It is choosing to give up something in order to turn your attention to God. This month, you are doing a type of fast whenever you give up foods other than rice and beans.

Fasting is not easy, so it's important to keep our focus on God and his purposes for the fast. But in these verses, God is talking to people who were mistreating others and getting into fights and arguments on the days they were fasting. Does that sound like their focus was on God? God reminds them that their fasting is supposed to provide help for people in need.

Fasting is also something that other people might notice and be curious about. Has anyone asked you any questions about the different food you're eating? What a great opportunity to talk to them about the real reason you're doing it! As we let God change the way we live, it gives other people a reason to turn their focus to God and to think about making changes in their lives, too.

Think of another family you could invite over to share a dinner of rice and beans with you, maybe a family that doesn't know much about Rice & Beans Month at all. It will be a great chance to spend some time with them and talk with them about why you are fasting. Who knows? They might feel inspired by God to join in as well!

What are some other ways that you can focus on God and focus on others as you fast? One great idea is to pray. Take some time as a family right now to pray for people who are hungry today.

PRAYER

God, teach us to be content with less, so that we have more to share with those in need. May our lives reflect the life of Jesus, who "was rich, yet for our sakes became poor." May we embrace the words of Paul: "I have learned the secret of being content in any and every situation, whether well fed or hungry, whether living in plenty or in want. I can do all this through him who gives me strength." Amen.

If I give all I possess to the poor and give over my body to hardship that I may boast, but do not have love, I gain nothing.

I Corinthians 13:3

One Sunday afternoon, my husband Keith and I played board games with our two daughters. The day had been lovely so far, and having some fun together enhanced the joyful atmosphere. It felt overwhelmingly wonderful to simply be a family. So wonderful, in fact, that the girls stood up after the last game and said, "Let's go clean our room!"

The girls' usual reasons for cleaning their room are: to earn screen time, to create a more welcoming environment for guests, or to preserve their mother's sanity. This was a new one. It seemed like they were inspired to do something that would build on the love and togetherness we had felt all afternoon. Same action (cleaning their room), different motivation (love).

After several years of eating rice and beans in March, I can say that my motivation has varied from year to year and sometimes from day to day. "It's good for the kids." "It will help me eat a cleaner diet." "Everyone else at Lahash is doing it." "It's a great way to set aside money for giving when our finances are tight." These are not terrible reasons. But they're not love, so they do not accomplish in me what only love is able to do.

Love reconnects me to that sense of family and togetherness. Love softens my heart, even to the point of breaking it. Love exposes the shallowness of my thinking, the limited scope of my faith. I begin to understand that God's vision goes beyond feeding the physically hungry. God wants to fill the deep hunger in every soul, and draw all of his children into deeper relationships with each other. He invites us to live in that joyful atmosphere where simply being a family is wonderful.

I have proven Paul's statement true far too many times. I have done good things with selfish motivation, and "gained nothing," just as he says. I want to pursue the opposite, with love as my motivation: *If I faithfully eat rice and beans, and give all my savings to the poor, and if I willingly choose this temporary hardship out of love for my brothers and sisters in Christ, I gain everything.*

Jen Johnson, Writer/Editor at Lahash
Portland, Oregon

FOR KIDS

Try acting out these two scenes as a family, and then answer the questions.

Scene 1

Lonely Lucas, *alone at recess*: I really wish I had a friend to play with today.

Selfish Susie: Hey, Lucas! Do you want to play catch with me?

Lonely Lucas: Sure, thanks!

(They play catch until recess is over, then walk back into school together.)

Lonely Lucas: Thanks, Susie. I was getting tired of being by myself at recess, but I've just felt kind of shy ever since I started coming to school here.

Selfish Susie: Yeah, no problem. So, I heard you just got a new trampoline. Why don't you ask your dad if I can come over and jump on it?

Scene 2

Lonely Lucas, *alone at recess*: I really wish I had a friend to play with today.

Caring Christa: Hey, Lucas! You look like you could use a friend. Come be on my kickball team!

Lonely Lucas: Ok, thanks!

(They play kickball until recess is over, then walk back into school together.)

Lonely Lucas: Thanks, Christa, that was so much fun!

Caring Christa: No problem. I was new at this school last year, so I know how it feels. I'm glad you're in our class now, but I know it's kind of hard to be new. You can play with me every recess if you want to!

Why did Susie play with Lucas? How do you think that made him feel? Why did Christa play with Lucas? How do you think that made him feel? Both girls played with Lucas, but for different reasons. God teaches us that it's not just doing good things that matter, but our reasons for doing them matter, too. Eating rice and beans so that we can share the money we save is a good thing to do. What are some important reasons for doing it?

PRAYER

Loving God, we confess the sin of spending our limited time on pointless pursuits that draw us away from you. Help us to see with your perspective and feel with your heart. Let our words and actions flow from the love you have poured into us. Guide us in our attempts to compassionately care for your most vulnerable children. Awaken our spirits to the impact of our daily choices, and receive our joyful worship even as we share this simple meal today. Amen.

Though the fig tree does not bud and there are no grapes on the vines,
though the olive crop fails and the fields produce no food,
though there are no sheep in the pen and no cattle in the stalls, yet I will
rejoice in the LORD, I will be joyful in God my Savior.
The Sovereign LORD is my strength; he makes my feet like the feet of a
deer, he enables me to tread on the heights.

Habakkuk 3:17–19

A s they gathered in the shade of a huge mango tree to evade the scorching mid-morning sun, I watched the East African church members greet one another warmly. Even though I was simply sitting in on their meeting as a guest, I was somewhat revered as an American preacher. Little did these people know that they would shortly be the ones teaching me a much-needed lesson.

The meeting ran long, as many meetings do. The pastor whispered in the ear of a young boy who then quickly disappeared. Ten minutes later, the boy returned with a helper, a crate of warm soda, and 20 packs of "biscuits" (cookies). I'm not a soda drinker, nor do I enjoy desserts much, so this snack held no appeal for me.

Each item was carefully distributed with a bow of the head, and the glass bottles were opened gently to make sure the loose cap was left on top. I had all kinds of things running through my mind as this was going on: *Soda is so bad for us. It shouldn't be served to people without offering a healthier choice. I don't even like soda; it's way too sweet. I've had these biscuits before. They taste kind of like Gerber baby cookies.*

A loud voice interrupted my thoughts saying we needed to rejoice in the Lord for the nourishment he had provided for us. This launched another round of internal dissent. In my estimation, these items were hardly considered nourishment. I was not particularly thankful for them. But the pastor's voice boomed on:

Oh, King of Glory, we thank you for your gracious provision. Oh my Master, in your hands are all things. You supply every good thing that we may always rejoice in you. Today we have been kept long in our work of serving you and this lovely congregation you have so graciously given us charge over. We have need of nourishment at this moment, oh King of Glory. Jehovah Jireh, we accept even this small blessing from your hand to strengthen us so that we may complete this meeting and bring glory to your name. The soda refreshes us in this heat. The biscuits give us energy for the next hour. Exalted Master, we receive them as representing the totality of your kindness toward us. In the everlasting name of Jesus, Amen.

And at that moment, I was schooled in reverent gratitude to God. I had been so quick to undervalue and even disdain the very same items that prompted the pastor's heartfelt prayer. In the sunburnt land of Northern Uganda, where drought damages crops and shrinks cattle to bones, the people understand Habakkuk's words well. And they rejoice in the Lord. They credit him always, finding their strength in him and thanking him for the smallest of gifts. How about you?

The Sovereign Lord is our strength. Let us rejoice in him in every circumstance, and thank him for every gift.

Clark Blakeman, Partnership Development Director at Lahash
Portland, Oregon

FOR KIDS

Imagine sitting down at the table for dinner and finding an empty plate in front of you. There is no food on the table, so you go to the kitchen. All the cupboards are empty. You look around town to find there's no food anywhere! What would you think? What would you say?

Habakkuk describes a similar situation in today's verses. How does *he* respond? Habakkuk chose to rejoice despite his dire situation, because God gave him strength! As we trust God more and more, we will be able to rejoice even in hard times. It's not easy! It takes a lot of practice. Instead of "fig trees and olive crops," let's put some other words in Habakkuk's prayer to help us practice:

Even though my best friend moved away,
Even though there are no kids in the neighborhood who are kind to me,
Even though I do not feel like I fit in at school,
Yet I will rejoice in the LORD, I will thank him for always being with me!
The LORD is my strength; he gives me power when I need it the most! Amen.

Try writing a similar prayer, using your own words:

Even though _____ *does not* _____ ,
Even though there are no _____ ,
Even though I do not _____ ,
Yet I will rejoice in the LORD, I will _____ !
The LORD is my strength; he _____ ! Amen.

PRAYER

God, open our hearts and minds to be challenged, humbled, and renewed by the example of our East African brothers and sisters in the faith. They are often rich where we are poor, wise where we are foolish, and thankful in situations that would find us discontent. Teach us, Lord, by their example, to see past the fleeting wealth and temporary troubles of this world, and instead to lift our eyes to you in thankful worship and joyful hope. May our sincere efforts on their behalf bless them as richly as they bless us. Amen.

We ought always to thank God for you, brothers and sisters, and rightly so, because your faith is growing more and more, and the love all of you have for one another is increasing. Therefore, among God's churches we boast about your perseverance and faith in all the persecutions and trials you are enduring.

II Thessalonians 1:3–4

When we practice spiritual disciplines like fasting, we hope to see evidence of God changing us to become more like Jesus in our hearts and actions. But what does that difference really look like? According to Paul's words to the Thessalonian church, the evidence is in growing faith and increasing love.

Take a moment to notice how your faith has already grown through this experience. As you sacrifice convenience and pleasure, are you aware of God meeting your needs in new ways? Perhaps your spiritual appetite is growing as your physical appetite is denied, or you are finding yourself drawn to prayer more often than usual. These are a few among many potential signs of a growing faith.

Many of us participate in Rice & Beans Month because of love for people who have big needs. How do you sense love increasing in you? Maybe you have more compassion toward those who live in poverty. You may be more aware of the impact your actions have on the poor. Are you finding yourself drawn to stories of suffering people around the world? Does your heart feel even more tender toward hurting children you have never met? It's pretty amazing to notice the unique ways that love is increasing in your life.

As you desire to see your faith grow and your love increase even more through this experience, pray for that specifically as you prepare to eat each meal.

Erin Holcomb, Lahash volunteer and child sponsor
Portland, Oregon

FOR KIDS

Have you ever prayed to God about something specific, and then received an answer? How did you feel when that happened? Your faith in God is planted deep in your spirit like a little seed planted in dirt. God wants that seed to grow and grow throughout your life, so that you have faith as HUGE as the tallest tree you have ever seen! Every time God answers your prayers, fills you with joy, speaks to your heart, encourages you through scripture, or helps you through a hard time, it's like he is caring for that little seed and causing your faith to grow.

As you eat rice and beans and then see how many people receive food because of your sacrifice, the seeds of faith inside you will grow a bit. As your faith grows bigger and bigger, you won't be able to stop yourself from sharing it with others, and that helps the faith inside them grow a little bit, too! You will also learn that even when God doesn't answer prayers in ways you can see, you can trust that he is always loving and faithful.

Mama Susan is a person whose seed of faith has grown into a strong tree even though she has experienced a lot of pain and struggle in life. She does her best to take care of many children, and has seen God provide for their needs again and again. Check out the video "Mama Susan's Tips" at *eatriceandbeans.com/video*. She gives us a few cooking ideas for Rice & Beans Month, and also reminds us how important this month is.

Afterward, have everyone at your table take a turn sharing an example of God answering a prayer. Let each story water your seed of faith and cause it to grow today!

PRAYER

F ather, thank you for providing for all our needs today, and especially for this food. We want to love you with everything in us, and we want our hearts to be shaped like yours. As we eat our rice and beans today, may our faith in you grow and our love for others increase, so that your work can be seen in and through us. Pour out on us the delight of being fully alive in your boundless agape love. In the name of Jesus, Amen.

"What should we do then?" the crowd asked. John answered, "Anyone who has two shirts should share with the one who has none, and anyone who has food should do the same."

Luke 3:10–11

This question from the crowd is prompted by John calling them a brood of vipers! This sounds a little harsh, doesn't it? He told them to produce fruit in keeping with repentance and to not just say to themselves, "We have Abraham as our father." In other words, their lives must change now that they have turned to God and want to be baptized. He finished by saying every tree that does not produce good fruit will be cut down and thrown into the fire. John definitely doesn't mince words!

"What should we do then?"

This question comes up again and again in Luke as the good news is preached. When tax collectors asked it, they were told to collect only what was required. When soldiers broached the question, they were told to stop extorting money and accusing people falsely, and to be content with their pay. This question puts hands and feet to our faith. The ways we use money and material possessions should be marked by the Father's love in visible ways.

As followers of Jesus, we have asked, "What should we do then?" and God has invited us to set aside this time to eat simply and share with those in need. Personally, I'm so much more aware of the excess I have in my life and the needs of my friends in East Africa when I eat in solidarity with them. I'm also more aware of the state of my heart. My challenge for each of us is that we continue to ask this question and listen to God during this journey. How is he calling you to change your life? How is he calling your faith to come alive and bear fruit?

Katie Nelson, Sponsorship Director at Lahash
Portland, Oregon

FOR KIDS

S ome people who wanted to follow God went to a teacher named John the Baptist and asked him what they should do. John could have said many things. He could have told them to pray more, to memorize scripture, or to tell other people about God. Those are all good things, but that's not what he said! John told them to look at the things God had given them. If someone had two shirts or extra food, that person should share with another person who doesn't have those things.

One way that you are learning to follow God is by helping to feed people who are hungry in Africa. Are there other ways you can share some of your "extras?" As a family, think of some ways you can share with others and do them this week!

PRAYER

G racious God, we want to hear your voice. As we set aside unnecessary foods, help us also to set aside the distractions that prevent our hearts from connecting with yours. Encourage and challenge us, Holy Spirit, as only you can. Help us release anything that is not worth holding onto, so that we can fully cling to you and respond to your work within us. Amen.

We continually ask God to fill you with the knowledge of his will through all the wisdom and understanding that the Spirit gives, so that you may live a life worthy of the Lord and please him in every way: bearing fruit in every good work, growing in the knowledge of God, being strengthened with all power according to his glorious might so that you may have great endurance and patience, and giving joyful thanks to the Father, who has qualified you to share in the inheritance of his holy people in the kingdom of light.

Colossians 1:9b–12

East African Christians know how to pray. If you have ever had the privilege of experiencing a church or prayer service with your African brothers and sisters, you know what I mean. Seldom-used words like "fervent" suddenly seem perfectly appropriate.

During a trip to Tanzania, I saw one of the local pastors laying a large tarp across part of the dusty floor of the church. "Pastor, what is that for?" I asked. His reply was simple. "Tonight is our prayer service." I was not making the connection. Noticing my puzzled look, he continued to explain. "This helps to keep our clothes from becoming dirty." It took a moment for the meaning of his words to sink in. So many people would be on their knees and faces before God in prayer that it was standard practice to lay down a tarp in preparation. I remember thinking, "These folks are serious about prayer."

Throughout that trip I continued to see prayers offered up with an intensity that could not be contained to a seated position. They showed me that prayer can be more bold, more passionate, and more integrated into every part of life than I ever imagined. I found myself longing to embrace the power of prayer as fully and freely as those I had witnessed. The experience was inspiring and unforgettable.

I know our East African friends are praying for us now, as we eat rice and beans together with them. As I read these verses from Colossians, I can hear them. I can see them standing up, eyes closed, hands raised. Their voices are clear and strong as they continually ask God to fill us during this time of fasting. Take a moment and read this scripture again. Know that the news of your act of love has reached your brothers and sisters. Be confident they are praying for you. Allow the Spirit to use their prayers to bring you strength, knowledge, endurance, and patience.

Now read the verses once more, this time as a prayer over the vulnerable in East Africa. Don't confine your prayers to a seated position, or to silent thoughts in your mind. Take a lesson from your neighbors and stand up tall or fall to your knees. Raise your hands and raise your voice. Read the verses aloud with boldness and passion. Let the Spirit connect you in true solidarity that crosses oceans, cultures, and languages in an instant. Drink in the sense of God's presence and linger there in the sweet unity of prayer.

As we join together in sharing a common meal, let us remember to share the deep connection of prayer as well. Let God draw our hearts together in this truth: the differences that divide us are not nearly as strong as the Spirit that unites us.

Casey Schilperoort, Media Director at Lahash
Portland, Oregon

FOR KIDS

On a globe or a map, find where you live. Then find the East African countries of Uganda, Tanzania, Kenya, and South Sudan. Have an adult help you figure out the distance between these two parts of the world.

If you sent a letter or a package to someone in East Africa, it would probably take over a week to get to them, maybe even two weeks or more. If you decided to travel there, it would require lots of driving and lots more flying, and would probably take at least two days. But if you contacted someone there through a phone call, you could connect with them right away!

We're going through a long process right now. We're eating rice and beans, then donating our saved money, and then Lahash will send the money to East Africa so that it can be used to buy food. It takes a while, much longer than sending a package. But PRAYER is more like a phone call; you can connect right away! As our friends in East Africa pray for us, God hears them instantly. And when you prayed those prayers in the devotion today, God heard you instantly. Through prayer, God connects our lives with our East African friends right now in this moment, even though we are very far apart.

PRAYER

We live to proclaim your name, Jesus! As you inspire us to action, may every good work bear fruit to feed a hungry world with your abundant love. Reveal your light in every face we see, until the light of your kingdom fills our vision. In every daily task and choice, help us to joyfully take hold of the life that is truly life. Amen.

Therefore, I urge you, brothers and sisters, in view of God's mercy, to offer your bodies as a living sacrifice, holy and pleasing to God—this is your true and proper worship. Do not conform to the pattern of this world, but be transformed by the renewing of your mind. Then you will be able to test and approve what God's will is—his good, pleasing and perfect will.

Romans 12:1–2

How much are we willing to give? That's a tough question, isn't it? Are we talking about money, time, energy, comfort, or what? Are we talking about eating rice and beans for a month? Oh wait, we're giving our whole lives ... *as a sacrifice?* This sounds unpleasant.

Sacrifices have been made by human cultures for centuries, for various reasons. Usually sacrifices involve something dying. Yet here we are exhorted to be a living sacrifice. That's a different definition of sacrifice than people are accustomed to. God gave himself, now he wants us to do the same. This sacrifice sets us free to live abundantly and courageously. His life for ours, now our life for his glory.

The reality is, we all sacrifice and give our lives for something. Perhaps it is for ourselves, other people, a cause we believe in, money, dreams, or comfort. By declaring with our heart, "Here I am, Lord; let your Spirit live through me and be my guide," we are yielding to a new way of sacrifice. The sacrifice becomes more alive than it was before. Offering our body as a sacrifice means making our whole self available for God's kingdom. Our life is offered as worship to the One who made us.

God shows us extravagant love and mercy through the life, death, and resurrection of Christ, inviting us from death to life. We respond by embracing and radiating his love wherever we are. Living like this is true worship, which God treasures and celebrates. As we intentionally choose to let God's Spirit shape our hearts and minds, we look and think differently from the ugly patterns of sin that have been repeated throughout history. We are transformed by God and gain true understanding of his will. Confidently knowing God's will comes through testing and trying it out as a transformed living sacrifice.

Being a living sacrifice is amazing and inspiring. In essence, God wants to live uniquely through you. As you live by the Spirit, you become a light to this world, proclaiming that you are God's beloved, and he is yours. Your life can be a powerful testimony of experiencing mercy and absolutely knowing you are loved. This brings a smile to God's face. So live for what matters. Live loved because you *are* loved, and the world is dying to know that they are, too.

Keith Johnson, Lahash volunteer and child sponsor
Portland, Oregon

One day, Samuel's teacher assigned an art project to the whole class, adding that they would be dismissed to head outside for some extra recess time as soon as they finished. The kids were excited about extra recess, and rushed sloppily through their art projects in a race to see who could get outside first. Samuel was the last student left in the classroom, working hard on a beautiful painting of a forest scene. His teacher asked, "Samuel, I know you love recess time, so can you tell me why you stayed in class to work so carefully when everyone else was hurrying out the door?"

"Well, Mr. Wilson, as soon as you told us about the project, I thought of my friend, Sara. She is really sick in the hospital right now, and she has to miss one of her favorite things, a camping trip with our whole church group. I just thought I could paint her a scene that would remind her of the woods, and hang it up in her hospital room for her, that's all."

Samuel's choice is a good example of what today's verse means when it says, "Do not conform to the pattern of this world, but be transformed by the renewing of your mind." The pattern of the kids in Samuel's class was to do careless work and race outside. But Samuel went in a different direction. The Holy Spirit within him turned his mind toward Sara, and he didn't really care what his other classmates were doing because he wanted to do something loving for his sick friend.

Can anyone in your family think of a time where they followed God's leading, instead of following the pattern of the world around them? Share as many examples as you can think of! They will be good reminders to continue letting God renew our minds and teach us to follow his guidance every day.

PRAYER

Holy God, we confess that we have conformed to the patterns of this world. In doing so, we have selfishly disregarded the needs of others and fallen away from you. We offer ourselves to you today. Forgive us by your grace, transform us with your truth, and strengthen us with compassion that we might bear the burdens of our brothers and sisters. In gratitude for your countless gifts, may we seek to embody your generous love. Amen.

DAY 12

This is how we know what love is: Jesus Christ laid down his life for us. And we ought to lay down our lives for our brothers and sisters. If anyone has material possessions and sees a brother or sister in need but has no pity on them, how can the love of God be in that person? Dear children, let us not love with words or speech but with actions and in truth.

I John 3:16–18

John, the writer of today's scripture, has a unique way of throwing your spirit into the air to float enraptured among the clouds at one moment, only to punch you in the gut at the next. For example, look at the opening of John's gospel:

Verses 1 and 4: *In the beginning was the Word, and the Word was with God, and the Word was God ... In him was life, and that life was the light of all human kind.* (Soaring!)

Verse 11: *He came to that which was his own, but his own did not receive him.* (Punched.)

And later, in Chapter 3:

Verse 17: *For God did not send his Son into the world to condemn the world, but to save the world through him.* (Floating on hope!)
Verse 19b: *... people loved darkness instead of light because their deeds were evil.* (Hope is dashed.)

This is the way John writes. Elevating Jesus so that the reader is drawn up with admiration, love, and hope. Then, before the elation is fully developed, slamming down the truth of humanity's brokenness, hard enough to knock the wind out of you. Today's passage follows suit:

This is how we know what love is: Jesus Christ laid down his life for us. (Floating!)

And we ought to lay down our lives for our brothers and sisters. (Here it comes ...)

If anyone has material possessions and sees a brother or sister in need but has no pity on them, how can the love of God be in that person? (Ouch. Direct hit.)

His question is sobering, but certainly not meant to prevent us from soaring again. This intentional season of simplicity fosters a reflective posture that lifts our spirits as we are used by God to lift up others. With our focus on Jesus, we are empowered to love the way he does: sacrificially. We are acknowledging our food abundance, seeing those without sufficient nutrition, and denying ourselves the delicacies we enjoy, thereby revealing the sacrificial love of God in us.

Take this month as an opportunity to "float with Jesus" a bit longer; to lay down your life for your brothers and sisters. Spend more time enraptured by the person of Jesus and in awe of his love rather than dwelling on your human frailty. Soar. Float. For, as the love of God soaks more deeply into you, you will exalt Christ. You will be lifted up yourself, and so will our precious friends in East Africa.

Clark Blakeman, Partnership Development Director at Lahash
Portland, Oregon

FOR KIDS

A ct out this scene with your family or friends: A man named Rich Ronnie is walking down the street. He has so much food that he is throwing some of it away after taking only one bite. Then he sees a hungry man named Poor Peter who wishes more than anything to eat the extra food that Rich Ronnie is throwing away. Rich Ronnie sees Poor Peter, but he doesn't care. He keeps all his food for himself, even throwing some in the trash as Poor Peter watches.

Is Rich Ronnie showing love like Jesus did? Act out the scene again, but this time, choose a different way for Rich Ronnie to act, a way that shows the love of Jesus. Read today's verses again, and notice words that describe the way Rich Ronnie acted the first time, and then the way he acted the second time.

PRAYER

G od, teach us to be content with less, so that we have more to share with those in need. May our lives reflect the life of Jesus, who "was rich, yet for our sakes became poor." May we embrace the words of Paul: "I have learned the secret of being content in any and every situation, whether well fed or hungry, whether living in plenty or in want. I can do all this through him who gives me strength." Amen.

The discerning heart seeks knowledge, but the mouth of a fool feeds on folly.
All the days of the oppressed are wretched, but the cheerful heart has a
continual feast.
Better a little with the fear of the LORD than great wealth with turmoil.
Better a meal of vegetables where there is love than a fattened calf with hatred.

Proverbs 15:14–17

"Y ou can't choose your circumstances, but you CAN choose your reaction to your circumstances." This is a mantra our family adopted after hearing it in a sermon a few years back. When flesh wages war with the Spirit, it serves as a gentle reminder to me—the mama—as well as to our children. People who are oppressed haven't chosen to endure such affliction, but did you notice that it is not the "non-oppressed person" who has a continual feast? Rather, it is the one who has a cheerful heart.

Can a person have a cheerful heart under dreadful conditions? Ask Paul and Silas, who sang at the top of their lungs in prison (Acts 16:16–40). Ask Corrie ten Boom, who watched her gentle sister Betsie thank God for the fleas in a concentration camp. (*The guards' aversion to the pests allowed the sisters to share the gospel with other oppressed women!*) Countless believers through the ages and today, by the overflow of God's grace in their lives, *choose* to remember that the JOY of the Lord is their strength. Despite wretched circumstances, they *choose* to feast on the fruit of the Spirit, fruit that will last (John 15:16). Despite having few physical comforts, they *choose* to fear the Lord rather than look for riches. And despite working with meager meal ingredients, we can *choose* to bask in the blessing of love.

Can you see the power of our choices? Even when we cannot control our circumstances, we can still control our reactions. By realizing what we can and cannot control, we move from victimhood to victory.

I find the first verse of today's scripture especially fascinating in light of our Rice & Beans Month experiences. "The discerning heart seeks knowledge, but the mouth of a fool feeds on folly." As followers of Jesus with a passion for reaching out to the vulnerable—the oppressed—we seek to know our Savior in a deeper and more intimate way. We are foolish if we choose to focus on our lack, dwelling on our own selfish desires. The temptation to feed our souls on the folly of temporal pleasures may come in the form of chocolate chip cookies or the momentary satisfaction of releasing our anger in all of its distasteful glory. Instead, may we choose to see the hand of God at work, and may God grant us discerning and cheerful hearts that we may continually feast on him.

Beverly Jacobson, Lahash child sponsor
Naples, Italy

FOR KIDS

hink about the last time you went to a birthday party or holiday celebration. Were there special foods to eat? Any games? What else made it fun? Now think about what it would have been like if you showed up, but nobody else was there. Same food, same games, but no special people to eat with or play with. What would that be like?

Friends and family are really important at a party! Actually, they're important any time, aren't they? During Rice & Beans Month, it is easy to think about food a lot because we're eating different things than usual. But as you think about your next meal, focus on being thankful to God for giving you such special people to share it with. Part of the scripture passage for today says, "Better a meal of vegetables where there is love than a fattened calf with hatred." That is a good reminder that it takes more than just food to make a meal wonderful. Being surrounded by people we love can bring joy to *any* meal!

As a family, take turns filling in these blanks to make a proverb similar to the one in today's passage:

Better a meal of_____ with the people I love
than eating_____ with people who don't like me.

Better to eat a meal of_____ with family and friends
than to eat _____ all alone.

PRAYER

oving God, we confess the sin of spending our limited time on pointless pursuits that draw us away from you. Help us to see with your perspective and feel with your heart. Let our words and actions flow from the love you have poured into us. Guide us in our attempts to compassionately care for your most vulnerable children. Awaken our spirits to the impact of our daily choices, and receive our joyful worship even as we share this simple meal today. Amen.

As Jesus started on his way, a man ran up to him and fell on his knees before him. "Good teacher," he asked, "what must I do to inherit eternal life?" "Why do you call me good?" Jesus answered. "No one is good—except God alone. You know the commandments: 'You shall not murder, you shall not commit adultery, you shall not steal, you shall not give false testimony, you shall not defraud, honor your father and mother.'"
"Teacher," he declared, "all these I have kept since I was a boy."
Jesus looked at him and loved him. "One thing you lack," he said. "Go, sell everything you have and give to the poor, and you will have treasure in heaven. Then come, follow me."
At this the man's face fell. He went away sad, because he had great wealth.
Mark 10:17–22

In this passage, a rich man runs up to Jesus and falls on his knees, desperate to know what he must do to inherit eternal life. Even though he has fulfilled all of the religious requirements and followed God's law since he was a child, he knows something is missing.

Jesus agrees. Something *is* missing.

"Go, sell everything you have and give to the poor … . Then come, follow me."

Even though the rich man's obedience would have a profound impact on the vulnerable, Mark makes it clear that Jesus is not instructing this action because of his concern for the poor. The reason behind Jesus' words, Mark writes, is that he "looked at him and loved him." If all Jesus cared about was providing for the poor, he could multiply loaves and fish or turn stones into bread.

Feeding the poor is not the real problem. Our hearts are the real problem. And the real potential. God is not simply concerned with money changing hands from those who have it to those who do not. He is concerned with money changing hearts by the power of his Spirit. It is so easy for us to focus on the transaction that we forget that what God really desires is transformation.

If God has stirred your heart to be involved with Rice & Beans Month, it is not because he needs your grocery money to help feed the poor. It is because he wants to transform you. God wants to shape your heart. He wants to break your addictions. He wants to teach you how to love more deeply.

He wants you to come and follow him.

Casey Schilperoort, Media Director at Lahash
Portland, Oregon

FOR KIDS

Before Jesus started going to different towns to teach people about the Kingdom of God, he gathered a group of people to go with him. They were his *disciples*, which basically meant they would get to be really good friends with Jesus and hang out with him all the time and learn from him every day. That sounds pretty great, right? But they had some decisions to make. They had jobs. They had families. They had houses. They had friends. If they decided to go on this Big Adventure with Jesus, they would have to leave those things behind for quite a while. But they did it, and their lives were changed forever because the Big Adventure with Jesus turned out to be super-amazing.

In today's verses, Jesus asks the rich man to make the same kind of choice. He had a lot of money and a lot of things that were very important to him. Jesus told him to sell all his stuff and give the money to help poor people. The man had a really hard time with that idea. If he would have realized how much more important Jesus was than all his money and stuff, he would have been ready to join the Big Adventure with Jesus, too. Based on how the story ends, what do you think the rich man decided? Why?

Draw a picture that shows Jesus and his disciples on a Big Adventure, with the rich man left behind with all of his money and his stuff. Think about Jesus giving you the same choice he gave all of them, and draw yourself into the picture to show your answer.

PRAYER

God, open our hearts and minds to be challenged, humbled, and renewed by the example of our East African brothers and sisters in the faith. They are often rich where we are poor, wise where we are foolish, and thankful in situations that would find us discontent. Teach us, Lord, by their example, to see past the fleeting wealth and temporary troubles of this world, and instead to lift our eyes to you in thankful worship and joyful hope. May our sincere efforts on their behalf bless them as richly as they bless us. Amen.

But godliness with contentment is great gain. For we brought nothing into the world, and we can take nothing out of it. But if we have food and clothing, we will be content with that.

I Timothy 6:6-8

Have you been noticing the lies? Maybe you're a bit more aware of them during this journey of eating simply. Messages all around us promise that life will be better, easier, and happier when we start indulging: "Just imagine how good it will be! You need this! You want this! You deserve this! You'll love the way you feel!" Whether it is eating dessert or buying new shampoo, contentment is always just around the next corner, one purchase away.

We know that true, lasting contentment is found only in the presence and service of God. But it is rare to get a quick fix from the lifelong journey of discipleship. Too often, we choose self-indulgence to feed our urgent craving to be in control. Jesus knew this. He told us it wasn't our job to provide for ourselves; God cares for the sparrows, the lilies, and our little bodies.

The Apostle Paul knew it, too. In this letter to Timothy, Paul writes a theology for the Christian lifestyle in one sentence. It's an easy formula, really: a God-seeker finds contentment in the beauty of living in God's service, fed and clothed by a generous Creator. There is simply nothing else to worry about.

Take a few moments today to reflect on your level of contentment. Is God meeting your needs? Are you content in his provision? There is real contentment available to us, but it doesn't survive in the world's formulas for happiness. We must confront the lies in our own hearts and replace them with the truth found in scripture. Only then will our hearts find true rest.

Erin Holcomb, Lahash volunteer and child sponsor
Portland, Oregon

FOR KIDS

Think of a toy or game that you really want. Really really REALLY want. What is so great about it? How would your life be different if you had it?

Today's verses remind us that toys, games, fun vacations, or other new things are not going to be with us for very long. They will be fun for a while, and then they will get old or break, or we will just get tired of them. That doesn't mean those things are bad; it just means we need to remember that they are not the most important things in our lives. If we love God and we learn to be content in his love for us, we have something that will last forever.

There will be many times in your life that you will really *really* want something. You might even think you NEED it in order to be happy. You will probably get some of those things, and you will not get some of those things. And you will have to decide in your own heart if you can be happy and content no matter what. With your family, talk about what it means to be content with what you have. Does it sound like something you can practice doing?

PRAYER

Father, thank you for providing for all our needs today, and especially for this food. We want to love you with everything in us, and we want our hearts to be shaped like yours. As we eat our rice and beans today, may our faith in you grow and our love for others increase, so that your work can be seen in and through us. Pour out on us the delight of being fully alive in your boundless agape love. In the name of Jesus, Amen.

DAY 16

Some wandered in desert wastelands,
   finding no way to a city where they could settle.
They were hungry and thirsty, and their lives ebbed away.
Then they cried out to the LORD in their trouble,
   and he delivered them from their distress.
He led them by a straight way to a city where they could settle.
Let them give thanks to the LORD for his unfailing love
   and his wonderful deeds for mankind,
for he satisfies the thirsty and fills the hungry with good things.

Psalm 107:4–9

For some of us, the past couple of weeks have been fairly easy. But for most of us, the experience has been difficult, and it has already tested the limits of our self-discipline and love. As we adjust to these alterations of our normal meal patterns, many of us feel hungry or thirsty at times.

Psalm 107 contains four stories of God displaying lovingkindness toward people in need. The one we read today describes people who wandered in a desert, hungry and thirsty with nowhere to settle. When they turned to God in distress, he mercifully delivered them.

Many brothers and sisters around the world are suffering at this very moment from hunger and thirst. Many are passionately breathing out whispered prayers for deliverance. We're taking one simple step toward identifying with these dear people, exploring the idea of solidarity. I pray that this experience is enlarging your ability to understand and love with compassion.

Feelings of gratitude may be a bit easier to come by at the end of this journey when we enjoy diverse food again. But let's not wait until then. We can rest assured that our hunger and thirst will be satisfied soon, so let's hold onto that promise for our brothers and sisters who have not yet seen it come to pass. In fact, let's rejoice that God, in his grace, is allowing our fast to help fulfill that promise. Let's enter into thanksgiving now, for what he is doing and what he will do. He is the creator and sustainer of all things, and he will deliver his beloved children from their distress.

Dan Holcomb, Executive Director of Lahash
Portland, Oregon

FOR KIDS

Solidarity is one of our themes as we eat rice and beans. When you want to be in solidarity with someone, you do something differently in your life to make it match someone else's a little bit more closely. We are choosing to limit what we eat so that our diet is similar to the diet of many people around the world who don't have access to the huge variety of foods that we do. We are eating simple meals, similar to what they eat. It is one thing to know in your mind that lots of people eat this every day, but by doing it ourselves, we are much more able to understand what it feels like.

Do you think solidarity is important? Why or why not? How do you think it might change the way you think about people who are often hungry and thirsty? Find the video called "Thank You from Joseph" at *eatriceandbeans.com/video*. A boy named Joseph talks about how his diet has changed because of people caring enough to eat rice and beans. (He speaks in Swahili, so make sure you have someone to read the subtitles to you if you need help.) Notice what his diet used to be like, and what it is now. How is it different from yours? As you continue to eat rice and beans, remember that you are showing solidarity with Joseph and many kids like him!

PRAYER

God, we thank you for your unfailing love and your wonderful deeds for all humankind! In body and in spirit, we know that you satisfy the thirsty and fill the hungry with good things. Too many of our brothers and sisters around the world, and specifically in East Africa, are struggling as they wait for the fulfillment of this promise. Thank you for the opportunity to join you in bringing this promise to life! May all your children find satisfaction for their thirst and fulfillment of their hunger, and may we help bring this to pass, through the rest of Rice & Beans Month and beyond. Amen.

Not only so, but we also glory in our sufferings, because we know that suffering produces perseverance; perseverance, character; and character, hope. And hope does not put us to shame, because God's love has been poured out into our hearts through the Holy Spirit, who has been given to us.

Romans 5:3–5

We had been sponsoring children through Lahash for many years when we decided that it was time for our family to meet one of our kids living in Northern Uganda. East Africa was beautiful: vast spaces, open skies, brilliant colors, and rust-tinted dirt that stuck to us like accidental tie-dye. As we shared everyday life with our East African brothers and sisters, we experienced and observed some of the hardships that they faced. Each day was plagued with back-breaking work, physical affliction, and an astounding lack of resources. They lived in profound poverty and suffered from preventable diseases. Yet every day there was laughter. There were smiles, songs, and joy. Our friends had a depth of perseverance, character, and hope that I both admired and craved.

Rice & Beans Month usually starts out exciting for us. Our family is hopeful and eager. We want to help our friends in East Africa, specifically our sponsored kids. We post their pictures on the wall next to a chart that tallies how much money we are saving for them. We are eager to share from our sacrifice. We are motivated by the idea of making a difference.

By the middle of the month, I realize that I am getting mad. I am mad at hunger. I am angry at the poverty that leads people to live hungry. At that point, *I am starting to get it.*

My soul aches for the hope and vision and joy that flows from our friends in East Africa. But their perseverance and character have not come easy. They have suffered. And, as I share a bit in their suffering, I have opportunity to receive the gift of character that only comes through affliction. God is their shelter and sustainer. God infuses our East African brothers and sisters with hope. As I embrace this chosen hunger as a gift, I find that Rice & Beans Month is less about our little family making a difference, and more about God and the *beautiful* that he weaves through suffering. And now I begin to worship.

Maybe Rice & Beans Month is not so much about food or poverty or hunger. Maybe this little bit of suffering, this chosen fast that often feels like claustrophobia in my own body, is the real gift.

India Main, Lahash child sponsor and traveler
Incirlik AB, Turkey

FOR KIDS

Riding a two-wheeled bike is a pretty great skill to have. But can you just wake up one morning and ride a two-wheeler perfectly if you haven't ever practiced before? Of course not! What are some of the smaller skills that you have to learn first, before you're ready for the big skill of bike-riding?

It takes some time to learn to pedal, balance, steer, watch for obstacles, speed up, slow down, and stop. Have you had any frustrations, or even crashes, when you practiced any of these skills? It might be really hard at times, but will you ever get to zoom around on a bike if you stop working on the skills?

"Perseverance" is a word from today's scripture that means to keep going and "stick to it" even when things are difficult. The Bible tells us that when we're facing a challenge, and we *persevere*, we become stronger on the inside, and God gives us the hope we need to continue trying. When we practice doing hard things with God in our hearts, we learn things about God and about ourselves that we would never have known if we stuck with only the easy stuff. So even when things are difficult, and you're sad or frustrated, remember that God is right there to give you the strength to persevere.

PRAYER

Gracious God, we want to hear your voice. As we set aside unnecessary foods, help us also to set aside the distractions that prevent our hearts from connecting with yours. Encourage and challenge us, Holy Spirit, as only you can. Help us release anything that is not worth holding onto, so that we can fully cling to you and respond to your work within us. Amen.

As for those who in the present age are rich, command them not to be haughty, or to set their hopes on the uncertainty of riches, but rather on God who richly provides us with everything for our enjoyment. They are to do good, to be rich in good works, generous, and ready to share, thus storing up for themselves the treasure of a good foundation for the future, so that they may take hold of the life that really is life.

I Timothy 6:17–19 (NRSV)

I was a young adult when a book with a stark, haunting title came out. *Rich Christians in an Age of Hunger* by Ron Sider. Now quite well-known, the title framed the dilemma of our age. The ancient themes of poverty and wealth (and their ability to erode community) are found throughout the Bible and are even more crucial to grapple with now. Our current age of materialism feels like wealth and poverty on steroids. I live in a culture where God's children diet because they overeat. Meanwhile, in many parts of the world, God's children struggle with malnutrition and disease, and far too many lose their lives to starvation. How do we care for each other in such an age, and what will be required?

Because of this awareness, our family lives in a small house in a low-income urban neighborhood. My children could list off their "deprivations." We buy mostly secondhand. We use one car. We use fans and not air-conditioning, dry our clothes on the line, and grow some of our food. In March, we do Rice & Beans Month.

So it was with some shock that I realized materialism had nonetheless taken root in me. Whether we focus on earning money to enjoy what it can buy, or on spending less and doing without, we are lured into thinking that money and possessions have the power to give us the life we want. Spending money or saving money can shelter the same demon.

It is easy, if we live on the affluent side of the equation, to set our hope on the fact that Rice & Beans Month will release thousands of dollars to care for the vulnerable. For those of us choosing a more modest way of living, it is easier to pride ourselves on the fact that the vulnerable benefit because of our standard of simplicity. Both are forms of materialism that fall far short of "the life that really is life."

Ultimately, these verses are not about money and riches; they are about liberation toward a life that is really worth living. That life is deeper, wider, fuller, and yes, at some level, oblivious to money because its hope is set "on God who richly provides us with everything for our enjoyment."

God wants for us a life that is not constricted or defined by wealth or poverty. All children of God can find some good works to do this day. We are all able to be generous of heart, ready to share. It is something we can choose, to enjoy the blessings God richly provides, and find the life that is really worth living.

Dee Dee Risher, writer and editor
Philadelphia, Pennsylvania

FOR KIDS

T hink about your bedroom for a minute. What things in there are most special to you? God's servant Paul looked at everything he had, and said that Jesus is so wonderful that even his very best things are like garbage compared to Jesus. Paul said that he wanted Jesus more than the nicest things that ANYONE had! (Philippians 3:7-9)

It is not wrong to have things that are special to us, and yet we need to remember that if we are looking to them for joy and security instead of looking to God, then "things" are in the wrong place in our lives. Having God's loving presence in our lives is the greatest blessing. All our "stuff" cannot compare!

Draw a picture of some of your favorite things, then draw a picture of Jesus. Which one is most important to you? Draw yourself next to what you chose. Take a photo of your artwork and email it to Lahash at *info@eatriceandbeans.com*.

PRAYER

W e live to proclaim your name, Jesus! As you inspire us to action, may every good work bear fruit to feed a hungry world with your abundant love. Reveal your light in every face we see, until the light of your kingdom fills our vision. In every daily task and choice, help us to joyfully take hold of the life that is truly life. Amen.

Bear one another's burdens, and in this way you will fulfill the law of Christ.

Galatians 6:2 (NRSV)

Have you ever been told you can change the life of someone in need? We hear it at church, see it on billboards, and read it in devotional books. It is inspiring to hear so many voices telling us we can make a difference for those being crushed under the burden of extreme poverty around the world. I believe those voices. For my family, participating in Rice & Beans Month is one way we are trying to change the lives of the poor in East Africa. But do I need the vulnerable to change my life? Do I even believe they can?

Today's scripture tells us to "bear one another's burdens." When I hear that phrase, I usually associate *bearing* with *removing*. The strong remove the burden from the weak. But what if bearing is less about *removing* and more about *receiving*? If we are supposed to bear each other's burdens, then why does my life look so burden-free while others are so weighed down? Part of the reason is that I would much rather change *their* lives instead of allowing them to change *mine*.

Now maybe this is just the rice and beans talking, but I think sometimes our checkbooks and bank accounts rob us. They rob us of the opportunity to share in the suffering and burdens of our brothers and sisters around the world. Our wealth can become a buffer that allows generosity to take place while preserving our comfortable lifestyles. We can raise a pen and write a check, hoping to remove the burden altogether, instead of bowing a shoulder to receive our share of the load.

Certainly God calls us to generously bless others with the resources he has given us. Sacrificial giving is a beautiful act of worship. But there is also something sacrificial, even worshipful, about receiving. As the weight shifts to lighten the load on our brother's shoulder, we find that it digs into our own. Suddenly we can feel it. It is uncomfortable. We are no longer observers but co-laborers, side-by-side under the burden. This entering in, this incarnation, was modeled by Jesus himself as he stooped to bear a burden that was crushing each of us. As we follow his example, we are engaging in the work of God's Kingdom alongside Christ who identified with the poor, the least, and the last.

I have grown to love it that Rice & Beans Month allows the vulnerable to change *my life*. In fact, it changes life for my whole family. It changes how we eat, spend our money, and prepare our meals. It affects our social and spiritual lives. It focuses our prayers and shifts our conversations. It helps us love the poor in a way that is so real we can actually taste it. We struggle a little bit more so our friends can struggle a little bit less. In the end, the giving becomes that much sweeter because the burden has been shared, and we have all been changed.

It is true that together we can change the lives of vulnerable children. And they can change ours as well.

Casey Schilperoort, Media Director at Lahash
Portland, Oregon

FOR KIDS

One time two girls named Leah and Kaya had a great idea. They wanted to make a giant leaf pile right under their porch so they could jump off the railing and land in it. The only problem was that there weren't very many leaves right under the porch! So they spread a big sheet underneath a tree with lots of fallen leaves, and raked and raked until the sheet was covered. When they folded up the corners of the sheet to make a sack, they realized that neither of them was strong enough to carry it! They could have emptied some of the leaves to make it lighter, but instead they folded the sheet so they could carry it together. By sharing the weight, they managed to carry the whole load to their pile.

Today's verse reminds us to "share the weight" of the problems in our lives. Sauda is a girl in East Africa who lives alone, and she used to wake up every day not knowing if there would be anything for her to eat. She had a lot of problems that were like heavy weights on her shoulders. Watch the video "Sauda's Story" at *eatriceandbeans.com/video* to see what happened when people decided to share her burdens!

Just like Leah and Kaya with the load of leaves, we can stick side-by-side with others and help them out. The load might still be heavy, but it makes a big difference when you have someone to carry it with you! Can you think of some things you are doing (or could do) to help kids like Sauda (or other kids you know) carry their load?

PRAYER

Holy God, we confess that we have conformed to the patterns of this world. In doing so, we have selfishly disregarded the needs of others and fallen away from you. We offer ourselves to you today. Forgive us by your grace, transform us with your truth, and strengthen us with compassion that we might bear the burdens of our brothers and sisters. In gratitude for your countless gifts, may we seek to embody your generous love. Amen.

I am not saying this because I am in need, for I have learned to be content whatever the circumstances. I know what it is to be in need, and I know what it is to have plenty. I have learned the secret of being content in any and every situation, whether well fed or hungry, whether living in plenty or in want. I can do all this through him who gives me strength.

Philippians 4:11–13

ecrets are tricky things often shrouded in mystery. Although Paul says in this passage that he can be content whether he is needy or overflowing, it didn't come naturally. Contentment was a secret that he had to learn.

Sometimes I find myself thinking that if I could live a little more like our East African brothers and sisters, then I would be more content. If only life were simpler. A little less materialism and a lot more relational living. But what about them, my friends across the ocean? Would they be more content with paved roads, dishwashers, and iced drinks? Do they crave my ease of transportation and grocery shopping? Would contentment be easier if they had more?

Paul said contentment was a secret, and it's revealed in these verses. Do you see it there? Paul says he can do it all *because of Christ*.

And there it is. The secret I so desperately need to know is that Christ redeems both the plenty and the want. Christ is here, and I can be satisfied, because this thing I'm currently living isn't all there is. There is HIM. Yes, yes! *He* is the secret who must be learned. And there is much more that has been written:

… in Christ is fullness of joy (Psalm 16:11)
… Christ in you is the hope of glory (Colossians 1:27)
… in Christ is freedom from condemnation (Romans 8:1)

In Christ.

As I live in this month's lack, this hunger, I sometimes find false comfort in the knowledge that I chose it, and it will end. I believe that this hollowness I feel is physical and temporary, and will soon be filled. But then the fast ends, and I discover that my real lack wasn't food. My relationships are fragile, my life is in chaos, and my heart feels hollow. I must seek the only source that can fill these needs. In Christ.

Saint Augustine, who was born in Africa and spent most of his life there, rightly prayed: "You have made us for yourself, O Lord, and our hearts are restless until they rest in you." But to rest in Christ when life is difficult, uncomfortable, painful, and confusing? To rest in Christ in the midst of a challenging fast? That's unnatural. My cravings must be *taught* to be satisfied with Christ, the one who is life and breath and everything. Resting in Christ, believing that in all circumstances it is HIM that I need most. This must be practiced not only during Rice & Beans Month, but throughout the journey of faith.

And that's the mystery. But let's not keep it to ourselves. Let's share this beautiful, wonderful, perspective-shifting secret.

India Main, Lahash child sponsor and traveler
Incirlik AB, Turkey

FOR KIDS

"I know a secret!" Those are very exciting words, no matter who says them. In these verses, a teacher named Paul says to his friends, "I know a secret" about how to be happy and content no matter if you have a little or a lot.

Do you know that secret also? To be "content" means to be satisfied and happy with the way things are. Do you know how to be happy, even if you don't have everything you want? Do you know how to be content, whether you're eating your favorite or least favorite food? Paul doesn't keep the secret to himself, he tells it in verse 13: "I can do all things through him who gives me strength." Paul doesn't try to be strong all on his own. He asks Jesus for strength to be content even when he is hungry or lacks the things he needs.

Think of a situation in your life that makes you feel jealous, unhappy, or like things just aren't fair. Maybe one of your friends hasn't been very nice lately, or you had to cancel an activity you were really looking forward to, or you were blamed for something that wasn't your fault. If you want, write down your example or draw a picture of it. Now draw a picture of Jesus whispering a secret into your ear. What does he say to give you the strength to be content in your situation?

PRAYER

God, teach us to be content with less, so that we have more to share with those in need. May our lives reflect the life of Jesus, who "was rich, yet for our sakes became poor." May we embrace the words of Paul: "I have learned the secret of being content in any and every situation, whether well fed or hungry, whether living in plenty or in want. I can do all this through him who gives me strength." Amen.

If you do away with the yoke of oppression, with the pointing finger and malicious talk, and if you spend yourselves in behalf of the hungry and satisfy the needs of the oppressed, then your light will rise in the darkness, and your night will become like the noonday. The LORD will guide you always; he will satisfy your needs in a sun-scorched land and will strengthen your frame. You will be like a well-watered garden, like a spring whose waters never fail.

Isaiah 58:9b–11

My two older children are starting to learn about money: earning it, saving it, and spending it. They now consider quite carefully whether any purchase is really worth it. They know that after they spend it, it's gone, so they had better be satisfied with what they bought!

I have always liked the English translation of these verses that says "spend yourselves…" Just like my kids are finding out with their money, we all have a certain amount of time, resources, strength, talents, and years on this earth. We are limited. We have to make decisions every day about how to spend ourselves. When you spend money, you choose a specific item or service to receive in return. What do you want to receive when you spend … *you*?

Too often, I spend myself on worthless things. Just like these verses mention, I yoke myself and others with the needless oppression of my expectations, I point my finger in judgment, and my hurtful and malicious inner dialogue slips out more often than I care to admit. All these things cost time and energy, yet leave me and others in darkness. What a waste.

Thankfully, God offers me the option to rise out of that darkness in brilliant light. He has plenty of investment opportunities with huge guaranteed returns. Spending myself on behalf of the vulnerable gets my focus off my struggles and my pointless judgments. It benefits people who need to experience God's love in practical ways, and allows me to partner with God in bringing his shalom to a broken world. In God's economy, spending myself somehow creates more riches!

Right now, that may mean that I need to take a few deep breaths after a new rice and beans recipe flops with my kids at the dinner table. It may mean navigating some awkward social situations to help others understand what we are (and are not) eating and why. It may mean that I repeatedly watch the videos of kids at the Lahash partnerships and just let the tears run down my cheeks as I pray.

As I consider the struggles of my brothers and sisters in Africa, the last two sentences of this passage are a perfect prayer. I desperately desire for them to experience the guidance of a loving God, for their needs to be met in a sun-scorched land, and for their bodies, souls, and spirits to be strengthened. I want the children at Lahash's partnerships to have actual gardens, well-watered and thriving, providing nourishing food. I want each of them to come to Jesus and drink, so that rivers of living water flow from within them (John 7:37–38).

The challenge I find in this passage is that I don't have much business proclaiming that prayer over them if I'm not willing to spend myself and partner with God to bring it about. This journey of eating simply will cost less money than we usually spend, but it costs us much more in other ways. Thank you, loving God, for the opportunity to spend ourselves in your kingdom here on earth.

Jen Johnson, Writer/Editor at Lahash
Portland, Oregon

FOR KIDS

Imagine that you and three friends go to an ice cream store, each with five dollars to spend. You hand the salesperson your money, and then you wait to see what you are given in return for your five dollars. You get a bag of apples! The second friend gives five dollars, and receives one shoe. The third person receives four boxes of pencils. The last friend gets a beach towel. Those are some strange things to end up with, especially when you wanted ice cream!

Is that how it usually works at a store? Of course not! When you spend money at a store, it pays for specific things that you pick out yourself. You don't give someone your money and take your chances on what they might give you back!

Just like with money, we spend our lives as well. We can spend our time and energy on lots of different things, and these verses are reminding us not to take our chances on what we might get. When we choose to spend our time and energy on the things Jesus cares about, we know for sure that our faith in him will grow and other people will get to feel Jesus' love for them through us. Does that seem like something that is worth spending yourself on?

Watch the video "A Special Nutrition Program" at *eatriceandbeans.com/video* to see what can happen when people spend themselves on helping kids in East Africa!

PRAYER

Loving God, we confess the sin of spending our limited time on pointless pursuits that draw us away from you. Help us to see with your perspective and feel with your heart. Let our words and actions flow from the love you have poured into us. Guide us in our attempts to compassionately care for your most vulnerable children. Awaken our spirits to the impact of our daily choices, and receive our joyful worship even as we share this simple meal today. Amen.

Therefore we do not lose heart. Though outwardly we are wasting away, yet inwardly we are being renewed day by day. For our light and momentary troubles are achieving for us an eternal glory that far outweighs them all. So we fix our eyes not on what is seen, but on what is unseen, since what is seen is temporary, but what is unseen is eternal.

II Corinthians 4:16–18

Without troubles, could we grow? Would we seek God? Our troubles shape us and give us opportunity to develop our faith by his grace.

I think about my brothers and sisters in East Africa who undergo intense troubles and trials, yet hold onto hope. There is so much beauty and strength in their joy. It is obvious that God's Holy Spirit is alive in them. Earlier in this chapter (verses 8-9), Paul speaks of being hard-pressed on every side, but not crushed; perplexed, but not in despair; persecuted, but not abandoned; struck down, but not destroyed.

I have seen this lived out. In the child who continues to smile, study hard, and praise God, despite losing his parents and facing stereotypes about the disease he struggles with. In the pastor who has seen so much corruption, pain, and injustice that he wrestles with God, yet continues to believe and trust in him. In the widow who worships her Savior with a grateful heart, even on the days that she cannot feed herself and her children.

What would it be like if my heart were truly focused on what is unseen instead of what is seen? How would my priorities, my perspective, and my attitude be different? Where is your heart's focus? As we eat in solidarity with our brothers and sisters in Africa, I pray that we take the opportunity to refocus our hearts and find joy and security in the unseen, trusting that eternal glory far outweighs the temporary struggles of this life.

Katie Nelson, Sponsorship Director at Lahash
Portland, Oregon

FOR KIDS

Imagine a big seesaw that works like a scale. On one side, you put a box with all your troubles in it. It's so heavy that you can barely even pick it up, and it holds one side of the seesaw down to the ground. But in these verses, God says that he is preparing a box of blessings for you that is WAY bigger and heavier than your box of troubles! Imagine God plunking down a big, huge box of amazing heavenly gifts on the other side of the seesaw. It's so heavy that it sends your box of troubles flying into the air, never to be seen again!

What are some of the troubles in your big, heavy box? What are some of the troubles in the big, heavy boxes of children in East Africa? Even though our troubles seem so heavy now, these verses remind us that they will come to an end, and God has blessings in store for us that will last *forever*. Even though we can't see all of those amazing blessings quite yet, we know that they weigh MUCH more and last MUCH longer than any of our troubles.

PRAYER

God, open our hearts and minds to be challenged, humbled, and renewed by the example of our East African brothers and sisters in the faith. They are often rich where we are poor, wise where we are foolish, and thankful in situations that would find us discontent. Teach us, Lord, by their example, to see past the fleeting wealth and temporary troubles of this world, and instead to lift our eyes to you in thankful worship and joyful hope. May our sincere efforts on their behalf bless them as richly as they bless us. Amen.

Do nothing out of selfish ambition or vain conceit. Rather, in humility value others above yourselves, not looking to your own interests but each of you to the interests of the others.

Philippians 2:3–4

R ice & Beans Month is a great time to share meals together, so I thought it would be nice to invite some old friends over for dinner.

Vanity arrived early (which impressed me very much). I half expected Selfishness to show up with a burger and soda. (He knows how much I love them.) But he politely sat down to a plate of rice and beans while remarking about how good it feels to be doing something so important. Humility was a little late, and honestly I forgot I had even invited him. He reminded me that we had talked briefly about sharing our meals together this month. It sounded vaguely familiar.

As we ate, Vanity paused between mouthfuls to tell me that I can make any-thing taste amazing. Selfishness just pushed his beans around while assuring me that my sacrifice this month was terribly impressive. Humility didn't say much during the meal, but thanked me sincerely when he finished. When he finally did speak, he reminded us of the kids in Uganda and of God's provision for them. He also asked me if I would tell some stories about the generosity and hospitality of my friends in Tanzania. Vanity was obviously uncomfortable and tried to quickly refocus the conversation back around me.

When we finished the meal, Selfishness offered all of us cookies for dessert. (Now that's the Selfishness I know!) As we were all choosing our cookies, I noticed Humility had left the room and that all of our plates had been cleared. He was in the kitchen washing the dishes. When he saw me, he asked if I would help dry them. I set my cookie down and picked up a towel. We talked about East Africa, we talked about God's love. I felt full. Not so much from the rice and beans but from something else.

I'm hoping Humility and I become better friends through this experience. I'm not so sure about Selfishness and Vanity, though. We used to have so much fun together, but lately we've been feeling kind of distant.

Casey Schilperoort, Media Director at Lahash
Portland, Oregon

FOR KIDS

W ho is the most important person in your life? Is it you? It is easy to want to be first in everything and always have the biggest and best. Today's verses say that we should seek out the best for the people around us, instead of just being interested in getting the best for ourselves.

Assign the characters from this devotion to people you are eating rice and beans with today. (Vanity, Selfishness, and Humility.) Try having a conversation as those characters, maybe with an adult's help. You could talk about eating rice and beans (like the devotion describes), or any other topic you can think of like playing a game, going shopping, or doing chores at home. Vanity and Selfishness say things that are focused on themselves, but Humility is focused on what is best for others.

In every day life, look for ways that you can put the needs or wants of others before your own. Maybe it means letting someone else go first on the swings, or letting them use the crayons you wanted. Remember the attitude of Humility; do these things for no other reason than sharing God's love with others.

PRAYER

F ather, thank you for providing for all our needs today, and especially for this food. We want to love you with everything in us, and we want our hearts to be shaped like yours. As we eat our rice and beans today, may our faith in you grow and our love for others increase, so that your work can be seen in and through us. Pour out on us the delight of being fully alive in your boundless agape love. In the name of Jesus, Amen.

...but now he [God] has promised, "Once more I will shake not only the earth but also the heavens." The words "once more" indicate the removing of what can be shaken—that is, created things—so that what cannot be shaken may remain. Therefore, since we are receiving a kingdom that cannot be shaken, let us be thankful, and so worship God acceptably with reverence and awe, for our "God is a consuming fire."

Hebrews 12:26b–29

There are two dramatic actions attributed to God in this passage: shaking and consuming by fire. God promises to shake the things of the world that can be shaken, leaving behind an unshakable kingdom for us. Unfortunately, I tend to put a lot of time and energy into filling my life with "shakable things." They're not necessarily horrible, evil, bad things. They're not necessarily good things, either. They're shakable things. Consumable, burnable, temporary things.

So when God goes about doing what God does—shaking and consuming—I have a lot to lose. The shaking and burning are uncomfortable, even painful. And not surprisingly, the process is ongoing. According to the passage, we are receiving this kingdom; it is not fully ours yet. God is a *consuming* fire, not a fire that once consumed and is now finished.

Even though the process is happening now, and it is not comfortable for me, the time to be thankful is now as well. What do I have to be thankful for? I get to live in this unshakable kingdom! I get to become more Christ-like as these shakable, burnable elements of my life are removed! My life is a journey of finding freedom from all the spiritual, material, and emotional junk that God can shake and consume. I have surrendered my life to a God who is actually capable of that. That leaves me in awe. Not because it is easy or because it feels good all the time, but because God loves me that dramatically. He wants me to live an unencumbered life. My acceptable, reverent, and authentically worshipful response is simply ... thankfulness.

In all honesty, true thankfulness does not come easily or consistently for me. Some days, just aiming for it is about the best I can manage. As I grow in this form of worship, I am amazed at how deeply it connects me to God and to my brothers and sisters in Christ. That experience of connection opens my eyes, offering a glimpse of that unshakable kingdom. I begin to see myself as God sees me, and I desire nothing more than to live fully and freely in communion with him.

Jen Johnson, Writer/Editor at Lahash
Portland, Oregon

FOR KIDS

Have you ever seen a snow globe? When it is sitting still, the bottom of the liquid-filled glass ball has a scene, maybe with people, buildings, and small trees, all covered in glittery snow. If you shake it, all the glitter floats around to look like a blizzard, but the scene is glued down so it can't be shaken loose.

Like a snow globe, some things in our lives are "shakable" like the glitter snow, and other things are "unshakable" like the scene. Many of our favorite foods have been shaken right out of our lives these days! But as we eat rice and beans and learn more about the needs of our friends in East Africa, we are gaining a heart full of love for people in other parts of the world who are hungry. We are also learning to have an attitude of thankfulness for the food we have. These are "unshakable" things that will stay glued into your life long after those other foods come back.

At *eatriceandbeans.com/video*, watch the video called "My Rice & Beans Experience." Several different people talk about the "unshakable things" that they learned through Rice & Beans Month! Then ask everyone in your family to name one or two "shakable things" in their life, and then one or two "unshakable things." Thank God together that he promises to fill our lives with unshakable things.

PRAYER

Gracious God, we want to hear your voice. As we set aside unnecessary foods, help us also to set aside the distractions that prevent our hearts from connecting with yours. Encourage and challenge us, Holy Spirit, as only you can. Help us release anything that is not worth holding onto, so that we can fully cling to you and respond to your work within us. Amen.

And whatever you do, whether in word or deed, do it all in the name of the Lord Jesus, giving thanks to God the Father through him.

Colossians 3:17

Pause for a moment and look back over the past year of your life. Of all the things you *did*, what stands out? There was probably some fun and excitement, a lot of normal daily life, and maybe you experienced some difficult things as well. Now what about all the different things you *said*? A lot of everyday conversation, some words that gave encouragement and hope to someone, and probably at least a few words that you wish you could take back. Just picking some standout moments from one year of life makes us realize that we all *do* and *say* a lot.

Whatever we do, we're called to do all of it in the name of Jesus. I find it interesting in this verse that not only deeds are considered "what we do." Words do something too; they are active, just like our deeds. Proverbs 18:21 says, "The tongue has the power of life and death." So knowing that both words and actions are important and full of potential, what does it mean to "Do it all in the name of Jesus?" I'm fairly certain that it *doesn't* mean we just start adding the words "in the name of Jesus" after each sentence or with each activity. I think the intention here is profoundly relational and personal.

I've always admired the life of Brother Lawrence, a monk who cultivated a rich walk with God while doing menial chores like washing dishes or peeling potatoes. He practiced dwelling in God's presence no matter what the day brought him. This has encouraged me through many unpleasant jobs. I've washed dishes in a student cafeteria, shoveled manure on a farm, and cleaned bathrooms in a bar. Talking with God gave me strength and peace as I was reminded of his nearness.

This verse in Colossians reminds us that doing all in Jesus' name is the fruit of cultivating a deep relationship with him. As we're led by his Spirit, we'll begin to look like him and sound like him, and our lives will reflect him to the world. We'll be filled with gratitude that we are alive in Christ and that our words and deeds have value, significance, and incredible possibility.

In all that we do, as we turn our hearts toward the Lord throughout the days we're given, God will transform us so that Christ shines through us and his name is magnified. For now, we've chosen to sacrifice our normal eating patterns so that others can find hope in the name of Jesus. The menial and mundane task of preparing rice and beans is laden with significance and infused with the presence of God. That sounds awesome. Thanks be to God!

Keith Johnson, Lahash volunteer and child sponsor
Portland, Oregon

FOR KIDS

Today's verse reminds us to do everything "in the name of Jesus." How do we do that?

To do something "in Jesus' name" means to do it in a way that honors who Jesus is and what he has done. Jesus doesn't live on this earth in his own body anymore, but he is alive in all of us who love him! So when we live in a way that shows other people who Jesus is, we are living "in Jesus' name."

The following sentences begin with something that is true about Jesus. Fill in the blanks with ideas of things you could say or do "in the name of Jesus." You can even add some more of your own fill-in-the-blank ideas!

Because Jesus *put the needs of others first,* I can *be patient when my little sister wants me to play with her.*

Because Jesus *cares for sick and hurting people,* I _____.

Because Jesus *is kind and loving,* I _____.

Because Jesus *forgives my sinful thoughts and actions,* I _____.

Because Jesus *is strong enough to defeat the power of evil,* I _____.

PRAYER

We live to proclaim your name, Jesus! As you inspire us to action, may every good work bear fruit to feed a hungry world with your abundant love. Reveal your light in every face we see, until the light of your kingdom fills our vision. In every daily task and choice, help us to joyfully take hold of the life that is truly life. Amen.

Each of you must give as you have made up your mind, not reluctantly or under compulsion, for God loves a cheerful giver. And God is able to provide you with every blessing in abundance, so that by always having enough of everything, you may share abundantly in every good work.

II Corinthians 9:7–8 (NRSV)

Our church decided to launch Rice & Beans Month with a free lunch for the entire church family after our morning worship service. Volunteers prepared twelve different dishes featuring rice and beans. Beside each dish we placed simple recipe cards that included the name of the dish, the ingredients, and how to prepare it at home.

In American culture, we are not used to eating rice and beans as staple foods. It is a challenge to adjust to eating this common meal in solidarity with our East African brothers and sisters. However, for our plates to more accurately resemble theirs, our dietary changes would have to be even more drastic.

For many years my family lived and ministered in a village on the South Coast of Kenya. Most of the people we knew often had only rice or beans, not both in the same meal. The rice would have small bits of stone, sticks, and dirt mixed in and the beans would be holey with worms or weevils or some other insect that beat me to my dinner.

Our friends rinsed the uncooked rice like they were panning for gold, swirling it in a dish until the rocks self-identified and could be carefully picked out. The raw beans were tossed in the air from a flat basket to allow leaves and other light material to blow away in the breeze. The beans were then soaked in water. Dead little black bugs floated to the top and were easily skimmed off.

Even after the meal was cooked and served, we still gently gummed the rice, knowing that hard chewing might cause a tooth to crack on a rock that slipped through quality control. And we squinted or looked sideways when we got fingers (no spoons) full of beans to our mouths. Sometimes it was just better not to clearly see what we were eating.

Thankfully, it is extremely rare to find dirt or bugs in my food here in America. But they are still present. Where? They resurface in my thoughts. The "dirt and bugs" are in my mind, not on my plate. The "dirt" on me is that I don't like sharing what is mine with a stranger. And I am "bugged" by having to alter my dietary choices day after day. Perhaps these struggles offer a clue as to why today's verses instruct us to settle the matter of generous giving in our minds.

The tension between selfishness and sharing is part of this journey, exposing my need for grace. After my mind has been set on sharing, I can cheerfully give to others and receive God's blessings in abundance. With God's help, may it be so.

Tom Smith, pastor of Silverton First Baptist Church
Silverton, Oregon

FOR KIDS

There are two big words in today's verses. Do you know what "reluctantly" means? What about "under compulsion?"

Have you ever done a chore you were asked to do, but made it very clear that you really didn't want to? Maybe you dragged your feet, complained, or had to be reminded several times. If so, you did that chore *reluctantly*.

Have you ever felt pressure to do something, because it was kind of important to get it done quickly? Maybe a homework project that was due the next day, or getting shots before traveling, or cleaning your room before grandparents arrive for a visit? If so, you did that *under compulsion*; you really had to get it done, like it or not.

God is telling us that when it comes to giving and sharing with others, he doesn't want us to do it *reluctantly* or *under compulsion*. We don't drag our feet and complain about it, and we don't give in to pressure as though we are doing it to avoid consequences. How does God want us to do it instead?

With your family, see if you can act out a scene where one person shares with another person *reluctantly* or *under compulsion*. Then change it up to show an example of giving cheerfully, from a thankful heart. And if you want to see an example of what it's like to cook rice and beans in Africa, watch the video "Cooking with Kabang" at *eatriceandbeans.com/video*. Kabang is a girl at Amazing Grace who often has the chore of cooking. What do you notice about her attitude?

PRAYER

Holy God, we confess that we have conformed to the patterns of this world. In doing so, we have selfishly disregarded the needs of others and fallen away from you. We offer ourselves to you today. Forgive us by your grace, transform us with your truth, and strengthen us with compassion that we might bear the burdens of our brothers and sisters. In gratitude for your countless gifts, may we seek to embody your generous love. Amen.

DAY 27

Be devoted to one another in love. Honor one another above yourselves. Never be lacking in zeal, but keep your spiritual fervor, serving the Lord. Be joyful in hope, patient in affliction, faithful in prayer. Share with the Lord's people who are in need. Practice hospitality.

Romans 12:10–13

We use the word *love* in so many ways that it loses meaning. "I love the 49ers." "I love your shirt." "I love you." In this passage, Paul says to "be devoted to one another in love." The word for *love* in the Greek is quite specific. He instructs Christians to *agape* one another, to have an unconditional, Christ-like love for others that requires action.

Take a moment to look at the actions listed here: honor, be zealous, serve, be joyful, be patient, pray faithfully, share with the needy, be hospitable. *Agape love* overflows into these actions. And this isn't a soft list of good ideas to pick and choose from; these are uncompromising standards for those who follow Jesus.

When life is comfortable I can bypass this passage quickly, but I have found that the challenge of eating rice and beans clarifies the motives of my heart: I seek pleasure, I like to meet my own needs first, and I am impatient. Something as simple as skipping dessert can bring my brokenness into sharp focus. This passage shows me how far off-target I really am.

So as I fast from my own urges, I find opportunities to exercise the very *agape love* that Paul describes. I can let my food cravings serve as reminders to pray faithfully for the kids that I sponsor. I can practice hospitality by inviting others to join me for a simple meal in my home rather than dinner out in a restaurant. I can be joyful in the hope that my small sacrifices will help provide both physical food and the good news of Jesus for kids who have gone without both. Thanks to eating rice and beans, the meaning of *love* suddenly becomes much richer.

Friends, let's spend some time right now meditating on Romans 12:10–13. Let's ask the Holy Spirit to show each of us how we can be more like Jesus today and put *agape love* into action in these specific ways. Let's commit to doing the hard work, and then let's celebrate the difficult and beautiful challenge of being transformed in the process.

Erin Holcomb, Lahash volunteer and child sponsor
Portland, Oregon

Have you ever poured water into a cup and accidentally filled it so full that it spilled over? When the cup couldn't hold any more, the extra water probably ended up on the table or the floor. God's love is like the water, and you are like the cup! God has so much love to pour into you that you can't hold it all. So how do you spill God's love onto other people?

Today's passage gives us some great ideas. Talk about each of these instructions from today's verses. What do they mean, and what are some ideas for how you actually do each of them?

Be joyful in hope

Be patient in affliction

Be faithful in prayer

Share with the Lord's people who are in need

Practice hospitality

Ask God to help you notice ways that you can spill his love today!

PRAYER

God, teach us to be content with less, so that we have more to share with those in need. May our lives reflect the life of Jesus, who "was rich, yet for our sakes became poor." May we embrace the words of Paul: "I have learned the secret of being content in any and every situation, whether well fed or hungry, whether living in plenty or in want. I can do all this through him who gives me strength." Amen.

Everyone felt a deep sense of awe, while many miracles and signs took place through the apostles. All the believers shared everything in common; they sold their possessions and goods and divided the proceeds among the fellowship according to individual need. Day after day they met by common consent in the Temple; they broke bread together in their homes, sharing meals with simple joy. They praised God continually and all the people respected them. Every day the Lord added to their number those who were finding salvation.

Acts 2:43–47 (Phillips)

A long time ago, Englishman J. B. Phillips wrote a book he called *The Young Church in Action.* It is a translation of Acts, the story of the earliest Christian church. He wrote a preface for his book that I love, and I want you to hear some of it:

Here we are seeing the early Church in its first youth, valiant and unspoiled–a body of ordinary men and women joined in an unconquerable fellowship never before seen on this earth.

No one can read this book without being convinced that there is Someone here at work besides mere human beings. … The Spirit of God found what surely He must always be seeking–a fellowship of men and women so united in love and faith that He can work in them and through them. … Never before has any small body of ordinary people so moved the world that their enemies could say, with tears of rage in their eyes, that these men 'have turned the world upside down.' (Acts 17:6)

One of the most amazing things about this group is that they totally shared their belongings. "Indeed, there was not a single person in need among them." (Acts 4:34) That's incredible, to be so full of the Holy Spirit that rich people share what they own, and poor people have all they need. A miracle!

That's really what Rice & Beans Month is about, isn't it? Maybe eating rice and beans has become a bit monotonous for us, even though we know that African kids eat simply all the time. Still, we keep at it, because the Holy Spirit not only reminds us to share, but also gives us the determination to continue sharing in this and many other ways, not only sharing the things we own, but also sharing ourselves. It's the way of the Holy Spirit, God's way. May this journey of Rice & Beans Month be a small but important step in sharing our whole lives, until J.B.

Phillips' description fits us as well: "a body of ordinary men and women joined in an unconquerable fellowship never before seen on this earth."

Jim Anderson, Lahash volunteer and child sponsor
Portland, Oregon

FOR KIDS

These verses from Acts describe the very first group of Christian believers who decided to follow Jesus together. What parts remind you of your life today? What parts sound really different?

We live in a different time, place, and culture than those first believers who lived so long ago, but the very same God they loved and worshipped is the God we love and worship today. They had the same Holy Spirit alive inside of them that we have. That means that even though our everyday lives might be different, God still wants us to love him and seek him and follow his guidance for how we live.

What are some things that God is guiding your family or your church to do to love and care for each other and to help people who are struggling in different ways?

PRAYER

Loving God, we confess the sin of spending our limited time on pointless pursuits that draw us away from you. Help us to see with your perspective and feel with your heart. Let our words and actions flow from the love you have poured into us. Guide us in our attempts to compassionately care for your most vulnerable children. Awaken our spirits to the impact of our daily choices, and receive our joyful worship even as we share this simple meal today. Amen.

For fools speak folly, their hearts are bent on evil:
They practice ungodliness and spread error concerning the LORD;
the hungry they leave empty and from the thirsty they withhold water.

Isaiah 32:6

One of the most consistent themes throughout the Bible is God's heart for the vulnerable. In this passage, it is evident exactly how seriously God considers our responsibility toward those who hunger and thirst. Depriving them is equated with evil, ungodliness, and spreading error concerning the Lord. When those of us who call ourselves followers of God do not work to alleviate hunger and thirst in the world, we are representing God poorly. We are offering an erroneous view of who God is and the way he loves.

The passage surrounding this verse contrasts the character of a fool with a ruler who is just. When justice reigns, shelter is provided for those who suffer. Their needs are met rather than denied. We've been moving toward justice together this month, making daily choices that have allowed us to set aside resources to help those in need.

As Rice & Beans Month draws to a close, we all face decisions about the way we will conduct our lives after we return to our normal eating patterns. Hopefully, this experience has given us a new and pervasive awareness of the needs of the world's hungry people and the role we play in alleviating those needs. We do not have to eat rice and beans year-round, but will *solidarity, simplicity,* and *sharing* continue with us into the rest of our year? How?

Let's remember God's heart for the hungry and thirsty while we peruse the stocked aisles of the grocery stores. Rather than focusing on which favorite foods to bring back first, let's consider how we will continue to be those who love justice. Are we a refuge for the vulnerable? Or fools who withhold from the needy?

Leisha Otieno, Partnership Development Coordinator at Lahash
Shirati, Tanzania

FOR KIDS

Lots of times in the Bible, God talks about the kinds of things foolish people do and what their character is like (what they are like on the inside). In today's verses, we find out that the foolish person wants hungry people to stay hungry and thirsty people to stay thirsty! Is that what God would want?

God doesn't want any of his children to be foolish, or to suffer every day because they lack food and water. One of the reasons we have been eating rice and beans is so that we can remember people who are hungry every single day. The money we saved by not buying more expensive groceries goes to help feed those hungry people.

Divide a piece of paper in half, and make a list with your family. On one side of the paper, list the hardest things about these past several weeks of eating rice and beans. On the other side, list the best things. What would a foolish person say about this list? What about a person who is following the ways of Jesus? What do YOU think? Is the hard list worth it because of the good list? Why or why not?

If you can, take a photo of your list and email it to *info@eatriceandbeans.com*. The Lahash team would love to see it and celebrate with you and your family for making it through the hard things in order to offer good things to our friends in East Africa!

PRAYER

God, open our hearts and minds to be challenged, humbled, and renewed by the example of our East African brothers and sisters in the faith. They are often rich where we are poor, wise where we are foolish, and thankful in situations that would find us discontent. Teach us, Lord, by their example, to see past the fleeting wealth and temporary troubles of this world, and instead to lift our eyes to you in thankful worship and joyful hope. May our sincere efforts on their behalf bless them as richly as they bless us. Amen.

Now he who supplies seed to the sower and bread for food will also supply and increase your store of seed and will enlarge the harvest of your righteousness. You will be enriched in every way so that you can be generous on every occasion, and through us your generosity will result in thanksgiving to God. This service that you perform is not only supplying the needs of the Lord's people but is also overflowing in many expressions of thanks to God.

Because of the service by which you have proved yourselves, others will praise God for the obedience that accompanies your confession of the gospel of Christ, and for your generosity in sharing with them and with everyone else. And in their prayers for you their hearts will go out to you, because of the surpassing grace God has given you. Thanks be to God for his indescribable gift!

II Corinthians 9:10–15

I s there a specific person who comes to mind when you think of the word *generous?* For me, it's my best friend whom I have known since childhood. She listens eagerly for God's direction regarding where her time, talents, and money should go. She's truly excited to hear what he has to say, and acts without hesitation.

At times she wonders why she is consistently blessed with abundant finances and a flexible schedule. I have a theory about this: *God enjoys entrusting her with money, time, and resources because he knows how freely and willingly she will use them for his kingdom!* I have told her, "Of course God pours all this into your life. You don't hang on to it! You're quick to release it wherever he directs. I bet God loves that."

As amazing as it is to see the needs of others being met by God through my friend's generosity, today's scripture reminds us that the meeting of needs is only half the picture. I love the verse that says, "not only supplying the needs of the Lord's people but also overflowing in many expressions of thanks to God." Paul is revealing the *full* picture: generosity and gratitude, overlapped and intertwined. Gratitude is such a profound part of this picture that it seems Paul can hardly find enough ways to describe it!

Our East African family exemplifies this interconnection. Anyone who has traveled there has undoubtedly been treated to a meal beautifully and sacrificially prepared. Out of deep thanks for the honor of hosting visitors, they selflessly offer the very best they can possibly provide, even if it means going without food themselves. Their material resources may be limited, but they draw from a rich spiritual harvest cultivated in faith.

Let's recount the ways *our* harvest has been enlarged on this journey. We have greater compassion, sharper awareness, deeper humility, and increased financial resources. God has enriched us in every way. Now is our opportunity to share selflessly and thankfully. Our loving and generous God invites us to become loving and generous bearers of his image. As the gifts begin to pour in, our entire international community will be "overflowing in many expressions of thanks to God." What an indescribable gift!

Jen Johnson, Writer/Editor at Lahash
Portland, Oregon

Please visit *eatriceandbeans.com/donate*
to share your savings with some truly thankful kids.

FOR KIDS

Eating some of your favorite foods again soon will be nice. It's easy to focus on that these days. But did you know that while your family has been eating rice and beans, money has been piling up little by little? And lots of other people have been eating rice and beans, so their money has been piling up, too!

Simple meals like the ones we've been eating don't cost as much as the foods we normally eat. So every time your family chose a simple meal, there was leftover money that was not used.

Guess what? It's almost time to use it! We've spent a lot of time learning about *simplicity* and *solidarity*, so let's get to the *SHARING!* Lahash is collecting money from everyone who participated in Rice & Beans Month, and then passing it along to families in East Africa who will be super-excited and thankful to receive food or to get help with starting gardens or raising animals. Isn't it amazing that we get to be a part of this?

Talk about how and when your family will send in your money to Lahash. Watch the video called "Thank You from the Kids!" at *eatriceandbeans.com/video* to see a lot of grateful kids who are eating healthier because of Rice & Beans Month. As a family, thank God for the opportunity to give!

PRAYER

Father, thank you for providing for all our needs today, and especially for this food. We want to love you with everything in us, and we want our hearts to be shaped like yours. As we eat our rice and beans today, may our faith in you grow and our love for others increase, so that your work can be seen in and through us. Pour out on us the delight of being fully alive in your boundless agape love. In the name of Jesus, Amen.

DAY 31

If you are participating for all 40 days of Lent, skip to page 88.

Then I heard what sounded like a great multitude, like the roar of rushing waters and like loud peals of thunder, shouting: "Hallelujah! For our Lord God Almighty reigns. Let us rejoice and be glad and give him glory! For the wedding of the Lamb has come, and his bride has made herself ready. Fine linen, bright and clean, was given her to wear." (Fine linen stands for the righteous acts of God's holy people.)

Then the angel said to me, "Write this: Blessed are those who are invited to the wedding supper of the Lamb!" And he added, "These are the true words of God."

Revelation 19:6–9

I have some friends who know how to throw a serious party. A seriously extravagant, joyful, magnificent party!

Every year our family heads to Salem, Oregon, for a beautiful nighttime Easter vigil. During the weekend of the vigil, we spend time with our friends Shep and Sharon Earl at their home. After the vigil ends (and we catch a few hours of sleep), we wake to delicious smells and the music of Handel's Messiah wafting through the home. Shep takes great pride in making sure the breakfast banquet is prepared perfectly. Sharon transforms their long table with decorations, chocolates, and sparkling juice. Sharon's kitchen and living room walls are covered in beautifully arranged crosses from around the world and church icons painted in rich colors. We sit down at this large table and exchange the words "He is Risen!" and "He is Risen Indeed!" We laugh and feast together as the sunlight breaks through the cherry blossoms outside the windows. It is one of my favorite moments of the year.

At the very end of the very last book of the Bible we are given a peek at another special feast.

Those redeemed by the blood of the Lamb are finally united with Christ in a cosmic wedding feast celebration. A period of human history marked by sin, disease, sadness, pain, loneliness, and death comes to a close. The most amazing Hallelujah Chorus ever performed bursts onto the scene! People from all regions of our planet and from all walks of life are united in a glorious party! We worship the King of all creatures and enjoy a delicious banquet together.

Today is also a day to celebrate! We've come through a time of fasting, sacrifice, and restraint as a community. We've submitted our desires and our patterns of life to Jesus and have let him shape us and grow us spiritually. Rice & Beans Month is officially over and now we get to share our savings with those in God's family who are truly hungry and thirsty. It is time to throw a party and enjoy a feast with friends!

Over the next few months I pray that your heart will be fixated on the great wedding feast of the Lamb. I pray that you will follow the Spirit's leading to fast, sacrifice, and practice appropriate restraint in anticipation of that amazing day. And I pray that in both times of sacrifice and celebration, your heart will stay tender toward our beautiful and vulnerable brothers and sisters around the world.

Dan Holcomb, Executive Director of Lahash
Portland, Oregon

FOR KIDS

We made it! Let's celebrate!
Someday God will gather ALL of his precious children from the WHOLE history of the world for a HUGE feast with Jesus. In the meantime, there are many things we can do today to prepare for that day. Learning to love God more and more, and becoming more and more generous with what we have are two important things we can do all throughout our lives.

As you imagine that great amazing beautiful feast with Jesus someday, draw a picture of eating a banquet with Jesus and his friends from around the world. If you can, take a photo of your artwork and email it to *info@eatriceandbeans.com*. The Lahash team would love to display it as a reminder of the greatest celebration of all!

PRAYER

Jesus, we rejoice today at the thought of feasting with you in heaven. Thank you for your death and resurrection. You have made it possible for us to be united with you in this life and beyond. You have been faithful to us through Rice & Beans Month, throughout our lives, and throughout history. We rejoice that your continued faithfulness will one day lead us to your banquet table to celebrate with all those who love you. As we enjoy an earthly feast to conclude our time of fasting, fill our hearts to overflowing with the hope of a victorious and eternal celebration with you. We love and worship you, our Risen King! Amen.

DAY 31

LENT

Is this the kind of fast I have chosen, only a day for people to humble themselves? Is it only for bowing one's head like a reed and for lying in sackcloth and ashes? Is that what you call a fast, a day acceptable to the LORD?

"Is not this the kind of fasting I have chosen: to loose the chains of injustice and untie the cords of the yoke, to set the oppressed free and break every yoke? Is it not to share your food with the hungry and to provide the poor wanderer with shelter—when you see the naked, to clothe them, and not to turn away from your own flesh and blood?"

Isaiah 58:5-7

Why do we fast? Why do we change our diets? It is a common thing to do during Lent, practiced for thousands of years by thousands and thousands of people. Thus, many fast food restaurants are promoting fish sandwiches right now for the benefit of those who are not eating meat. Giving up foods is pretty normal, but asking why we are giving up those foods is not.

Isaiah, in this powerful and challenging passage, asks us to think about why God would want us to fast. Sometimes we fast because it makes us feel special and different, and even better or more holy than other people. We choose to give up something and turn away from our physical desires, and then equate this with pleasing God because we are denying ourselves. This scripture makes it clear that we don't need to put on a show for God. God doesn't want us to fast for our own "holiness." God wants us to fast so that justice can be done. If we are eating rice and beans in hopes of receiving a "gold star," we miss the point of the fast and ignore the real reason for doing it.

Let's talk about why we fast. We fast to consume less. Rice and beans use fewer resources to fill our bellies than steak and fresh fruit from the other side of the planet. Through this fast we are bringing God's justice to the earth. When we give away the money we save to feed others who are hungry, we are bringing God's justice to other people.

Justice is something that we should all desire and work for. May this fast bring about God's redemptive work, in your heart and in the world.

Bob Brown, pastor of Stahl Mennonite Church
Johnstown, Pennsylvania

FOR KIDS

As a family, you have been fasting for a while now. Take some time to talk about these questions and think about how fasting has affected each of you: What have been *your* personal reasons for fasting during Lent? Have your reasons changed at all since you first started, or has it been the same reasons the whole time?

The writer of today's devotion ends with a blessing: "May this fast bring about God's redemptive work, in your heart and in the world." What does that mean to you? Do you sense God working in your heart in this Lenten season? How? And what about in the world, do you think our fasting will affect the bigger world around us? How?

PRAYER

Gracious God, we want to hear your voice. As we set aside unnecessary foods, help us also to set aside the distractions that prevent our hearts from connecting with yours. Encourage and challenge us, Holy Spirit, as only you can. Help us release anything that is not worth holding onto, so that we can fully cling to you and respond to your work within us. Amen.

For today's devotional, take some time to read and reflect on the following passage from the gospel of Luke.

S omeone in the crowd said to him, "Teacher, tell my brother to divide the inheritance with me." Jesus replied, "Man, who appointed me a judge or an arbiter between you?" Then he said to them, "Watch out! Be on your guard against all kinds of greed; life does not consist in an abundance of possessions."

And he told them this parable:

> *The ground of a certain rich man yielded an abundant harvest. He thought to himself, "What shall I do? I have no place to store my crops."*
>
> *Then he said, "This is what I'll do. I will tear down my barns and build bigger ones, and there I will store my surplus grain. And I'll say to myself, 'You have plenty of grain laid up for many years. Take life easy; eat, drink and be merry.'"*
>
> *But God said to him, "You fool! This very night your life will be demanded from you. Then who will get what you have prepared for yourself?"*

This is how it will be with whoever stores up things for themselves but is not rich toward God.

Luke 12:13–21

FOR KIDS

W hen the man in Jesus' story had a lot of extra grain, his idea was to figure out how to store and keep it for himself. Most of us probably don't have a lot of extra crops sitting around, so we don't really need to build big storage barns. But are we ever selfish in similar ways? If we have extra money, clothes, toys, books, or electronics, we probably don't build a barn, but we might try to rearrange our closets and shelves to fit everything. Whether from friends, stores, or ads we see, we get a lot of messages telling us that it's important to have a lot of stuff. When we listen to all of those messages, we get stuck in the same kind of thinking as the rich man Jesus describes.

Let's see if we can figure out what Jesus most wants us to learn from this story. If you look back at the very first sentence of the passage, you'll notice that someone in the crowd asked Jesus to do something very specific. What did that person want Jesus to do? How did Jesus answer that request? Why do you think Jesus did not do what the person told him to do?

Now if you look at the end of the passage, you'll find an interesting sentence that ends with a phrase that we don't really use very often: "rich toward God." Talk about this a bit as a family, and take a few quiet moments to think about it prayerfully. What do these words of Jesus mean to you today? Can you think of any other ideas for what we could do with extra stuff?

PRAYER

We live to proclaim your name, Jesus! As you inspire us to action, may every good work bear fruit to feed a hungry world with your abundant love. Reveal your light in every face we see, until the light of your kingdom fills our vision. In every daily task and choice, help us to joyfully take hold of the life that is truly life. Amen.

DAY 33

Start children off on the way they should go, and even when they are old they will not turn from it.

Proverbs 22:6

LENT

The picture below is of two amazing kids. One is Khadijah. She is a beautiful and energetic little girl who lives in a small home in Tanzania. Her mother is HIV-positive, and sadly, so is Khadijah. The medication that she takes to control the disease is only effective in combination with a nutritious diet. But because Khadijah's family has little money, at times they cannot afford to eat more than one meal a day, and the food they do eat is extremely basic.

Our family has the privilege of sponsoring Khadijah, and during Rice & Beans Month we also have the privilege of simplifying our diet so we can help improve hers. Part of the donated money provides a lunch program for Khadijah and other children who are battling the effects of HIV. Several days a week, they go to the local church and receive a nutritious meal which gives their young bodies the chance to grow and thrive in spite of their disease. Just by eating simple meals and sharing our grocery savings, Khadijah's life is dramatically impacted. I am amazed at what can be accomplished while sitting at the kitchen table.

The other child is my son, Asher. He is a beautiful and energetic little boy who lives in a small (by American standards) home in Portland, Oregon. He is healthy and enjoys three nutritious meals a day, plus snacks. During Rice & Beans Month, Asher will still eat some peanut butter and jelly sandwiches, yogurt, and cheese sticks. But for dinner every night, he will eat a simple meal of rice and beans. He doesn't like that menu much, but he makes it through. We explain how it allows us to share our money and love with Khadijah and others in need. We ask God to provide food for the hungry, and we thank him for ours.

At times we wonder if any of it is sinking in. But then we catch a glimpse. It may happen at dinnertime or before bed—sometimes even months later—but he remembers to pray for Khadijah and our friends who don't have food. When I hear those simple, sweet prayers, I realize that these intentional meals are shaping and expanding his young heart.

Yes, this fast has its challenges, but God has used it to change us. We say we want to love our neighbors and care for the poor and vulnerable. We say we want to pass on these values to our children. Rice & Beans Month puts all of that right in front of our family, so close we can literally touch, smell, and taste it. We pray it is doing the same for yours.

Casey Schilperoort, Media Director at Lahash
Portland, Oregon

FOR KIDS

K hadijah and the other kids who attend the Nutrition Program are very thankful to have those meals, because at home they often have very little food or no food. Does one good meal a day sound like enough? It is helping them A LOT, but there is still a long way to go to help the children and their families have enough food for ALL their meals EVERY day.

Rice & Beans Month is one way that God is using all of us to help provide for these children. Because God is using you in this way already while you're young, it's pretty amazing to think of all the many ways he will teach you to be loving and compassionate to others throughout your whole life!

Together with your family, take a few moments to pray for hungry children who are struggling with diseases in their bodies. Pray that God will continue to encourage their hearts and provide for their needs, and that our fast can be one of the ways God answers their prayers and takes care of them. Pray that God will continue to show you and your family many ways to love and care for others.

PRAYER

H oly God, we confess that we have conformed to the patterns of this world. In doing so, we have selfishly disregarded the needs of others and fallen away from you. We offer ourselves to you today. Forgive us by your grace, transform us with your truth, and strengthen us with compassion that we might bear the burdens of our brothers and sisters. In gratitude for your countless gifts, may we seek to embody your generous love. Amen.

Jesus, full of the Holy Spirit, left the Jordan and was led by the Spirit into the wilderness, where for forty days he was tempted by the devil. He ate nothing during those days, and at the end of them he was hungry.

Luke 4:1–2

W hy on earth would God Himself embrace a season of fasting? It might be because He knows some deep truths about the world and about humanity. God's decision again and again to give up His power – from when He came to earth in the form of a crying baby, to when He fasted in the desert, to when He allowed people to torture and execute Him – teaches us something very important: the world will not be changed when we ascend to power. God's Kingdom will not be furthered because an evangelical Christian resides in the White House or the highest court in the land. God changes the world through humility and service. It is a subversive tactic, yet highly effective. ...

The same truth applies to each of us on a personal level. We will experience radical transformation in humility and service, not superiority and power. The primary reason why we struggle so deeply to be transformed into the character of Christ is likely because so often instead of living with humility and vulnerability, we are busy chasing power and prestige.

Can we embrace the truths of Christ if we do not embrace His posture? His hands were exposed to disease and leprosy as He touched the sick. His knee bent to the ground to wash the sullied feet of His friends. His eyes lifted in prayer to the Father. His body bowed and was broken in death. As we learn to march in step with our Savior, we find that our swagger gives way to a lowly and humble way of walking.

To be strong Christians, we must embrace weakness. It is when we accept our humanity, when we are humbled by our fallibility, when we live vulnerably, that God is strong within us. Jesus was lowly, humble, even despised. He did not seek comfort. He did not even have a place to lay His head. He had every opportunity to pursue power yet didn't. The world systems and its currency did not hold value for Jesus. He had a vision of a different sort of kingdom.

Chris Seay, pastor of Ecclesia Houston
Houston, Texas

*The above devotional is an excerpt from the introduction of Chris Seay's book, **A Place At The Table: 40 Days of Solidarity with the Poor**, published in 2012 by Baker Books, Grand Rapids, MI. ©2012 Chris Seay, www.chrisseay.net*

FOR KIDS

The word "vulnerable" is used a lot in this book. Most of the time it is used to describe our East African brothers and sisters who are struggling with hunger and poverty. In this devotion, the word "vulnerable" is used in a different way. Talk about this with your family. What are the two different meanings of this word? When someone is vulnerable, does that mean they need help? Do you think it's better to try to be vulnerable or to avoid being vulnerable?

These are tricky questions, on purpose! Hopefully they will get you talking and thinking about this important word and the different meanings it can have. The way we understand this word will have a big effect on how we live our lives as followers of Jesus.

Watch "Reflections by Bethany Schlacter" at *eatriceandbeans.com/video*. Bethany shows us what it's been like for her to eat rice and beans, and she also shares some of the ways God has taught her and changed her through the experience, which is exactly what this devotion is talking about! Bethany has grown and become more and more like Jesus through this fast. Hopefully, she will encourage you as you become more like Jesus, too!

PRAYER

God, teach us to be content with less, so that we have more to share with those in need. May our lives reflect the life of Jesus, who "was rich, yet for our sakes became poor." May we embrace the words of Paul: "I have learned the secret of being content in any and every situation, whether well fed or hungry, whether living in plenty or in want. I can do all this through him who gives me strength." Amen.

DAY 35

LENT

Keep falsehood and lies far from me; give me neither poverty nor riches, but give me only my daily bread. Otherwise, I may have too much and disown you and say, 'Who is the LORD?' Or I may become poor and steal, and so dishonor the name of my God.

Proverbs 30:8–9

As we continue our journey through a season of simplicity, I'm struggling with contentment. I hate the extremes of poverty or riches. Under such unbalanced conditions, I vacillate between melancholy navel-gazing and arrogant boasting.

During every other month of the year, I live a good, comfortable life. I have ample food, clothing, shelter, clean running water, medical care, and educational opportunities. I don't worry about my safety. I live in abundance, and sometimes that troubles me. It can be easy to slide into a spiritual amnesia that says, "Who is the Lord?"

But can I tell you what scares me more than abundance? Lack. As soon as a bit of lack enters my daily life, I feel immediately that I don't have enough. I hate feeling hungry all the time, and I miss the freedom of food choices. In my ache for more, I feel a greedy coveting creeping in my soul. It focuses on what is missing and dishonors what God has provided.

But in Philippians 4:12–13, Paul writes, "I have learned the secret of being content in any and every situation, whether well fed or hungry, whether living in plenty or in want. I can do all this through him who gives me strength." Paul had been both needy and well-supplied, and in both he said that he had learned to be content! Contentment. I want that.

In her book *One Thousand Gifts,* Ann Voskamp says, "Contentment is never a matter of circumstances; contentment is always a state of communion, a daily embracing of God."

And isn't that it, friends? My pleasure, satisfaction, fulfillment—yes, my *contentment*—rests in Jesus who is the same yesterday, today and forever. My health, friends, and provisions may change, but the God who is good, and does good, never changes. This is his provision: *himself.* And this is what I must *learn*: to rest, trust, and be filled with God himself.

During this season of lack, I invite a balance into my otherwise unbalanced existence. This chosen fast is an invitation to remember the Giver, our kind God who is generous and tender and delights in giving us our daily bread. Our loving God wants us to see that he is enough, in any extreme or circumstance.

India Main, Lahash child sponsor and traveler
Incirlik AB, Turkey

FOR KIDS

oday's scripture passage talks about the dangers of having too much or too little. In your life, what do you think is more of a danger? How do you think the writer of this devotion would answer that same question? How do you think an extremely poor family in East Africa might answer that question?

For those of us participating in this fast, it is not likely that we struggle with poverty the way our friends in East Africa do. But when we give up something that we really like, it can be really hard! Right away, we feel terrible without it, even if it's not something we truly need. For example, we might be having a hard time without some of our favorite foods while we're eating rice and beans. We might really miss a favorite toy or game if it is broken or lost. We get so used to having these things that it feels hard to go without them.

Whenever the Bible talks about "daily bread," it usually means something like "what we need for today." If you made a list of "what I need for today" and a hungry child in East Africa made a list of "what I need for today," do you think the lists would be the same? What might be the same, and what might be different?

PRAYER

oving God, we confess the sin of spending our limited time on pointless pursuits that draw us away from you. Help us to see with your perspective and feel with your heart. Let our words and actions flow from the love you have poured into us. Guide us in our attempts to compassionately care for your most vulnerable children. Awaken our spirits to the impact of our daily choices, and receive our joyful worship even as we share this simple meal today. Amen.

For today's devotional, take some time to read and reflect on the following passage from the gospel of Luke.

hen Jesus said to his disciples: "Therefore I tell you, do not worry about your life, what you will eat; or about your body, what you will wear. For life is more than food, and the body more than clothes. Consider the ravens: They do not sow or reap, they have no storeroom or barn; yet God feeds them. And how much more valuable you are than birds! Who of you by worrying can add a single hour to your life? Since you cannot do this very little thing, why do you worry about the rest?

"Consider how the wild flowers grow. They do not labor or spin. Yet I tell you, not even Solomon in all his splendor was dressed like one of these. If that is how God clothes the grass of the field, which is here today, and tomorrow is thrown into the fire, how much more will he clothe you—you of little faith! And do not set your heart on what you will eat or drink; do not worry about it. For the pagan world runs after all such things, and your Father knows that you need them. But seek his kingdom, and these things will be given to you as well.

"Do not be afraid, little flock, for your Father has been pleased to give you the kingdom. Sell your possessions and give to the poor. Provide purses for yourselves that will not wear out, a treasure in heaven that will never fail, where no thief comes near and no moth destroys. For where your treasure is, there your heart will be also."

Luke 12:22–34

FOR KIDS

o you ever worry? What kinds of things do you worry about? Think about the feelings you have when you're worried. Sometimes it is hard to fall asleep, or you might cry or get angry more easily than normal, or you might have a tummy ache and feel like you can't eat anything. It can be hard to enjoy activities that normally are fun to you, because you just keep thinking about that one thing over and over again.

In today's verses, Jesus gives us lots of reasons *not* to worry. Picture your worries like a dry sponge inside you. Have everyone in your family choose a favorite sentence or phrase from these words of Jesus, and read it out loud a few times in a row. Picture that every time the words are repeated, it's like Jesus is dripping water onto that dry sponge. As you keep listening to his words, your worries are completely soaked with the water of his love and care. Whenever you feel that dry sponge of worry inside you, remember that Jesus wants to drench it with his words and set you free from your worries!

PRAYER

God, open our hearts and minds to be challenged, humbled, and renewed by the example of our East African brothers and sisters in the faith. They are often rich where we are poor, wise where we are foolish, and thankful in situations that would find us discontent. Teach us, Lord, by their example, to see past the fleeting wealth and temporary troubles of this world, and instead to lift our eyes to you in thankful worship and joyful hope. May our sincere efforts on their behalf bless them as richly as they bless us. Amen.

*Woe to those who make unjust laws, to those who issue oppressive decrees,
to deprive the poor of their rights and withhold justice from the oppressed
of my people, making widows their prey and robbing the fatherless. What
will you do on the day of reckoning, when disaster comes from afar? To
whom will you run for help? Where will you leave your riches? Nothing
will remain but to cringe among the captives or fall among the slain.*

Isaiah 10:1–4a

*In chapter six of Ron Sider's book **Rich Christians in an Age of Hunger,** he uses today's passage
as well as many others to show God's perspective on unfair systems and oppressive societal and legal
structures. The following section follows a discussion of "social sin" in which he explores what it
means for us to take responsibility for our part in these structures:*

U nderstanding the biblical concept of social sin is essential to understanding the seriousness of unfair systems. At the same time, honest discussion
should not leave people wallowing in guilt or feeling burdened to correct
every global evil.

The proper response to sin is repentance. And genuine repentance leads
to unconditional, divine forgiveness. Whenever we become aware of conscious
participation in unjust systems, we should ask God's forgiveness. God does not
want us to feel or be guilty; he wants us to be forgiven. He wants us to rejoice in
grace – and, in the power of the Spirit, to live differently.

However, living differently – doing all God wants us to do to change struc-
tural injustice – by no means involves trying to do everything. We each have
our own unique gifts and calling. God wants many of us to fast and pray about
social sin. Most should study, and many should write and speak out. Some should
join and support organizations promoting social justice. Others should run for
political office. All of us should ask how changes in our personal lifestyle could
help model a better world. But God does not want anyone to feel guilty for not
doing everything – or for taking time off for relaxation and recreation. Everyone
should prayerfully ask God what limited, specific things God wants him or her
to concentrate on. It was God, after all, who made us finite with only twenty-four
hours each day. Being called to do all God wants us to do to correct social sin
is not a heavy burden. It is an invitation to joy and meaning in life, an occasion
for blessing our neighbors, and a wondrous opportunity to be a coworker with
the Lord of history.

*Ronald J. Sider, Senior Distinguished Professor of Theology, Holistic Ministry,
and Public Policy at Palmer Seminary at Eastern University
King of Prussia, Pennsylvania*

FOR KIDS

ometimes when you stop to think about all the sadness and sickness and terrible situations in the world, it can be pretty overwhelming. All the world's problems can feel like a heavy weight on our hearts and minds. The writer of today's devotional has something to say about that. With your parents, talk about these important ideas from the last paragraph:

"We each have our own unique gifts and calling."

"... God does not want anyone to feel guilty for not doing everything ..."

Is there anything about these words (or any other part of the devotion) that encourages or comforts you?

God is inviting all of us to find joy in life, to bless our neighbors, and to be his partners and helpers in the world. We have been doing those things during this fast, and now it will be coming to an end in just a few days. But God's invitation doesn't end! So are you ready to see what's next in your family's unique calling? Take some time to talk and pray about this together.

PRAYER

ather, thank you for providing for all our needs today, and especially for this food. We want to love you with everything in us, and we want our hearts to be shaped like yours. As we eat our rice and beans today, may our faith in you grow and our love for others increase, so that your work can be seen in and through us. Pour out on us the delight of being fully alive in your boundless agape love. In the name of Jesus, Amen.

Today's devotional is an excerpt from chapter six of Ronald J. Sider's book
Rich Christians in an Age of Hunger: Moving from Affluence to Generosity, *published in 1997 by Thomas Nelson Publishers' W Publishing Group ©1997. www.wpublishinggroup.com.*

DAY 38
LENT

Grace and peace to you from God our Father and the Lord Jesus Christ. I thank my God every time I remember you. In all my prayers for all of you, I always pray with joy because of your partnership in the gospel from the first day until now, being confident of this, that he who began a good work in you will carry it on to completion until the day of Christ Jesus.

Philippians 1:2–6

Paul wrote the above words in a letter to the church at Philippi, eager to tell them how thankful he was for their partnership. In much the same spirit, the Lahash staff received the following letter from Esther Muhagachi, the Director of Grace and Healing Ministry in Dodoma, Tanzania:

Every Friday, the kids supported by Grace & Healing Ministry of Dodoma (GHMD) meet at the church for learning and socializing together with other kids. Part of the Friday program always includes having lunch together. We discovered that not only were most of the kids coming from very poor families, but that the only good meal they ate was at the church on Fridays. We became especially concerned for those infected with HIV. But we thank God for the people who fasted and joined the idea of eating rice and beans to serve these vulnerable kids who could not afford even a single meal a day. When we received the Rice & Beans Month money from Lahash, we decided to create a special Nutrition Program for the kids with HIV.

This special lunch is served to 28 kids at the church every Tuesday, Wednesday, and Thursday. Then on Friday they join all the others and eat together. It has been a blessing to many kids such as Paskali and Gabriel to mention a few, whose condition was worse due to HIV-related infections and lack of food while on antiretroviral drugs.

We have seen a difference and their condition has improved a lot. For example Paskali was kind of confused, you could find him picking food in a dumping place, and he was not going to school! But now he is able to go to school instead of searching for food, because he knows that by afternoon he will be at the church for lunch. For Gabriel, his grandmother had given up on him, waiting for his death. But due to the Nutrition Program his health has improved, and he is happily going to school.

There is much to tell about the Nutrition Program, but my heart is full of thanks for the Rice & Beans Month since this is a source of blessing to the GHMD kids. Thank you all who joined this program. You have fulfilled the word of God from Matthew 25:35, "I was hungry and you gave me something to eat."

My prayer for you comes from Isaiah 58:10, "And if you spend yourself on behalf of the hungry and satisfy the needs of the oppressed, then your light will rise in the darkness, and your night will become like the noonday."

Thank you and God bless you,

Esther EB Muhagachi, Director of Grace & Healing Ministry
Dodoma, Tanzania

FOR KIDS

The Nutrition Program that Mama Esther is talking about would not have been possible without people choosing to eat rice and beans and share the money they saved. There are two videos at *eatriceandbeans.com/video* that show even more about this program: "More Than A Meal" and "A Special Nutrition Program." If you haven't seen them yet, check them out!

The staff at Lahash's partner organizations in East Africa are always very thankful when God provides a way for them to help the vulnerable kids and families in their communities. They are thankful, AND they continue to pray for God to provide even more. What can we learn from them? Can we be thankful for the opportunity to eat rice and beans and help so many people, AND start to think about how we can do something more? We don't have to eat rice and beans every day forever, there are lots of different ways to be involved with helping people who are in need!

And if you need a little encouragement to get through these last few days of eating rice and beans, listen to Mama Esther's words in the short video "Encouragement from Mama Esther" at *eatriceandbeans.com/video.* You can make it!

PRAYER

Gracious God, we want to hear your voice. As we set aside unnecessary foods, help us also to set aside the distractions that prevent our hearts from connecting with yours. Encourage and challenge us, Holy Spirit, as only you can. Help us release anything that is not worth holding onto, so that we can fully cling to you and respond to your work within us. Amen.

LENT

For today's devotional, take some time to read and reflect on the following passage from the gospel of Matthew.

When the Son of Man comes in his glory, and all the angels with him, he will sit on his glorious throne. All the nations will be gathered before him, and he will separate the people one from another as a shepherd separates the sheep from the goats. He will put the sheep on his right and the goats on his left.

"Then the King will say to those on his right, 'Come, you who are blessed by my Father; take your inheritance, the kingdom prepared for you since the creation of the world. For I was hungry and you gave me something to eat, I was thirsty and you gave me something to drink, I was a stranger and you invited me in, I needed clothes and you clothed me, I was sick and you looked after me, I was in prison and you came to visit me.'

"Then the righteous will answer him, 'Lord, when did we see you hungry and feed you, or thirsty and give you something to drink? When did we see you a stranger and invite you in, or needing clothes and clothe you? When did we see you sick or in prison and go to visit you?'

"The King will reply, 'Truly I tell you, whatever you did for one of the least of these brothers and sisters of mine, you did for me.'

"Then he will say to those on his left, 'Depart from me, you who are cursed, into the eternal fire prepared for the devil and his angels. For I was hungry and you gave me nothing to eat, I was thirsty and you gave me nothing to drink, I was a stranger and you did not invite me in, I needed clothes and you did not clothe me, I was sick and in prison and you did not look after me.'

"They also will answer, 'Lord, when did we see you hungry or thirsty or a stranger or needing clothes or sick or in prison, and did not help you?'

"He will reply, 'Truly I tell you, whatever you did not do for one of the least of these, you did not do for me.'"

Matthew 25:31–45

FOR KIDS

When Jesus wanted to teach people about the Kingdom of God, he often used parables. Parables were stories that Jesus thought of, and they are full of ideas and examples to help people understand important lessons. Today's passage is one of those parables. Jesus describes two groups of people that made different decisions about how to treat others who were in need. One group did its best to help and show kindness; the other group did not. But both groups of people had a similar question for Jesus; something Jesus said didn't quite make sense to them. What was it? What do you think Jesus most wants them all to understand?

You have probably already realized that God gives all of us MANY things. Usually we think of God as the Giver and ourselves as the receivers. And that is often true! But have you ever thought about giving to God? Jesus is telling us through this parable that we can actually GIVE to HIM! What a cool thought!

Act out this parable as a family. One or two people can be *in need*: sick, hungry, or in prison. Someone else can act out the response of those on Jesus' right, and then those on Jesus' left. Have the *in need* people explain how it felt to be treated each time, and imagine that Jesus is the one speaking through them and telling you how it felt for HIM to be treated like that. So if we want to give something back to Jesus to show how thankful we are for his many gifts to us, what can we give? How can we give it?

PRAYER

We live to proclaim your name, Jesus! As you inspire us to action, may every good work bear fruit to feed a hungry world with your abundant love. Reveal your light in every face we see, until the light of your kingdom fills our vision. In every daily task and choice, help us to joyfully take hold of the life that is truly life. Amen.

Then I heard what sounded like a great multitude, like the roar of rushing waters and like loud peals of thunder, shouting: "Hallelujah! For our Lord God Almighty reigns. Let us rejoice and be glad and give him glory! For the wedding of the Lamb has come, and his bride has made herself ready. Fine linen, bright and clean, was given her to wear." (Fine linen stands for the righteous acts of God's holy people.)

Then the angel said to me, "Write this: Blessed are those who are invited to the wedding supper of the Lamb!" And he added, "These are the true words of God."

Revelation 19:6–9

I have some friends who know how to throw a serious party. A seriously extravagant, joyful, magnificent party!

Every year our family heads to Salem, Oregon, for a beautiful nighttime Easter vigil. During the weekend of the vigil, we spend time with our friends Shep and Sharon Earl at their home. After the vigil ends (and we catch a few hours of sleep), we wake to delicious smells and the music of Handel's Messiah wafting through the home. Shep takes great pride in making sure the breakfast banquet is prepared perfectly. Sharon transforms their long table with decorations, chocolates, and sparkling juice. Sharon's kitchen and living room walls are covered in beautifully arranged crosses from around the world and church icons painted in rich colors. We sit down at this large table and exchange the words "He is Risen!" and "He is Risen Indeed!" We laugh and feast together as the sunlight breaks through the cherry blossoms outside the windows. It is one of my favorite moments of the year.

At the very end of the very last book of the Bible we are given a peek at another special feast.

Those redeemed by the blood of the Lamb are finally united with Christ in a cosmic wedding feast celebration. A period of human history marked by sin, disease, sadness, pain, loneliness, and death comes to a close. The most amazing Hallelujah Chorus ever performed bursts onto the scene! People from all regions of our planet and from all walks of life are united in a glorious party! We worship the King of all creatures and enjoy a delicious banquet together.

Today is also a day to celebrate! We've come through a time of fasting, sacrifice, and restraint as a community. We've submitted our desires and our patterns of life to Jesus and have let him shape us and grow us spiritually. Rice & Beans Month is officially over and now we get to share our savings with those in God's family who are truly hungry and thirsty. It is time to throw a party and enjoy a feast with friends!

Over the next few months I pray that your heart will be fixated on the great wedding feast of the Lamb. I pray that you will follow the Spirit's leading to fast, sacrifice, and practice appropriate restraint in anticipation of that amazing day. And I pray that in both times of sacrifice and celebration, your heart will stay tender toward our beautiful and vulnerable brothers and sisters around the world.

Dan Holcomb, Executive Director of Lahash
Portland, Oregon

FOR KIDS

We made it! Let's celebrate!
Someday God will gather ALL of his precious children from the WHOLE history of the world for a HUGE feast with Jesus. In the meantime, there are many things we can do today to prepare for that day. Learning to love God more and more, and becoming more and more generous with what we have are two important things we can do all throughout our lives.

As you imagine that great amazing beautiful feast with Jesus someday, draw a picture of eating a banquet with Jesus and his friends from around the world. If you can, take a photo of your artwork and email it to *info@eatriceandbeans.com*. The Lahash team would love to display it as a reminder of the greatest celebration of all!

PRAYER

Jesus, we rejoice today at the thought of feasting with you in heaven. Thank you for your death and resurrection. You have made it possible for us to be united with you in this life and beyond. You have been faithful to us through Rice & Beans Month, throughout our lives, and throughout history. We can rejoice that your continued faithfulness will one day lead us to your banquet table to celebrate with all those who love you. As we enjoy an earthly feast to conclude our time of fasting, fill our hearts to overflowing with the hope of a victorious and eternal celebration with you. We love and worship you, our Risen King! Amen.

STORIES

The following articles were written and published from 2010 to 2014, during the first five years of Rice & Beans Month.

FILLING SAUDA'S PLATE

BY LEISHA ADAMS

Since 2009, Lahash staff member Leisha (Adams) Otieno has been living in Tanzania, where she experienced the inaugural Rice & Beans Month in a very personal way. Here, she shares how the month impacted Sauda, a child in Lahash's Sponsorship Program.

S auda is HIV-positive. Her mother died years ago from HIV-related illness and her father went to another city to look for work.

Her father built a house with four apartments. She lived in one, and there were tenants in the other three. He intended for those tenants to give Sauda rent money every month, and with that money she could pay for school fees and food. Unfortunately, it didn't work out that way. Immediately after her father left, the tenants stopped paying rent because she was a young girl. They just flat refused.

In March of 2010, we were able to enroll Sauda in the Sponsorship Program. At that time, all of the sponsors and other friends of Lahash were invited to participate in an event we were calling Rice & Beans Month. We asked everyone to eat simple meals of rice and beans for the entire month to express solidarity with our friends in East Africa.

All the people who participated in Rice & Beans Month sent in the money that they had saved on groceries, and we bought food for the families of kids in the program. We bought 15 pounds of beans for every child and 55 pounds of *unga* (maize flour). Those are the main staples of East African families' diets.

Some of the families had a lot of people living in their houses, and that food may only have lasted a few days. But Sauda lived alone and that was all the food that she had. The bag of unga lasted her more than a month, eating it for breakfast and dinner, and the beans lasted her at least a month as well. Before receiving that assistance, Sauda definitely went without food on some days. She would go to bed completely hungry because she didn't have any way to provide for herself.

It is amazing to be part of a Sponsorship Program that says, "We'll look out for you," and then to witness friends in the States eating simple meals in order to donate for Sauda's care. We were able to take the food that was purchased as a direct result of people changing their eating habits, and put it into the hands of a girl who was looking at going to bed hungry that night. That's a miracle in a lot of ways.

I know it isn't easy to eat a steady diet of rice and beans. When I moved to Tanzania, I started eating rice and beans pretty much every day. I know it takes a lot of getting used to. But being here, I see the benefit for the local people. I really feel privileged to be in the middle. I know what it costs people in America to do this, and at the same time, I know the huge impact it's having on girls like Sauda who need that nutrition.

In those times during Rice & Beans Month when it feels too difficult to have one more day of boring food when you could be eating any number of things, I wish you could be here with Sauda. I wish that she could cook you rice and beans. Rice and beans that she has because you've eaten rice and beans. It comes full circle.

I hope the story of Sauda will encourage you on those days when you want a cheeseburger or lasagna or enchiladas. Press on, knowing that your sacrifice means a lot to Sauda. ■

Sauda cooks beans provided by Rice & Beans Month.

TO WATCH A VIDEO OF SAUDA'S STORY, VISIT
EATRICEANDBEANS.COM

PLEASE PASS THE
SOLIDARITY

BY JEN JOHNSON

One Oregon family's Rice & Beans Month Experience

O ur girls were ages four and five in 2010, the first time we participated in Rice & Beans Month. We tailored our family's participation to suit them best, and to reinforce the themes of *simplicity, solidarity,* and *sharing. Simplicity* was a new word for them, but its meaning became clear as we sat down to our first meal of rice and beans. *Sharing* was an easy concept to build on. With preschoolers, it was already a daily topic of conversation. *Solidarity* was more of a stretch. My favorite quote came in a prayer by our four-year-old: "Thank you that we can have simple meals and that we can have a good time with solidarity." She then offered to scoop some solidarity onto several people's plates.

Ultimately, we knew that concepts such as solidarity, compassion, and empathy would need to be experienced, not explained. During that month, we intentionally spent time learning about the lives of kids their ages in East Africa. *What is the same? What is different? How would you feel about this simple meal if you had no other food today? What are the most important things that kids everywhere need?*

Our girls have never been to Africa, yet God has used the conversations, prayers, videos, and photos to connect their hearts with African kids. I truly cannot find words to express what that means to me as a parent and Christ-follower. Rice and beans was not the girls' favorite meal that year. It probably won't be in the future, either. That's okay. Especially when I consider that the simple choice to alter our normal eating patterns for just one month can have an immeasurable impact on each of us as well as on our East African family. ∎

MY

Three Different

RICE & BEANS

Perspectives

MONTH

On One Common Meal

EXPERIENCE

A lot of people are drawn to the *concept* of Rice & Beans Month.

**Simple Diet + Solidarity with the Hungry
+ Donating Extra \$\$\$ = Great Idea!**

Then there's the tricky part. *Actually eating* a simpler diet. For a month. From sensitive stomachs to picky children to busy lifestyles, there are many potential obstacles. With creativity, grace, and some trial-and-error, the following folks found ways to make it work. Let their ideas inspire you to do the same!

Rod and Lin Willett
Baby boomer couple, busy work schedules

Heading into our fourth year of participation, our goal is for each evening meal to be some variation of rice and beans, while meditating on the simplicity of life and the needs of our African brothers and sisters. What began as a "sacrifice" has opened up our lives to a much more healthful eating style, causing us to embrace more vegetables and legumes in our diet year-round.

Rod enjoys publicizing the month on Twitter. Each day he tweets something like, "Day 10 of www.eatriceandbeans.com. Today we are having jasmine rice topped with beans seasoned with broccoli and Thai sauce." In 2013, we hosted a large dinner party to introduce our friends to some delicious recipes. We are looking forward to participating again. At the end of March, it is so rewarding to tally up our savings and send that money to Lahash.

Bethany Campbell
Full-time 5ᵗʰ grade teacher

I enjoy cooking, but I don't always have time during the week. Quick meals are key for me. The crockpot is a big time-saver as it allows dry beans to soak and cook throughout the day, so they are ready to eat when I get home. I mostly eat black, pinto, or kidney beans mixed with veggies, over rice. Another favorite is burritos with salsa, cheese, or avocado for variety. My first year, I tried sticking to rice and beans for all my meals, but breakfast was a real challenge. I've switched to eating plain oatmeal for breakfast. Still cheap, and more filling than rice.

My best resource is the people around me who participate as well. It's definitely encouraging to share recipes, tips, and check in with one another. The Rice & Beans Facebook Page is a source for new recipes or cooking tips, along with encouraging stories from Lahash's partners in Uganda and Tanzania. For me, this is an opportunity to engage in advocacy and participate in a bigger story. I enjoy the challenge of eating simply, knowing that I am standing in solidarity with children and other believers halfway across the world.

Kevin and Rachelle Webster
Married, both working full-time

We try to make rice and beans the focus of lunch and dinner, adding in other goodies like vegetables, salsa, sour cream, and avocado. Things that have helped us are using a slow cooker and sharing meals with friends. Each year our goal is to only eat rice and beans, but we don't stick to it 100%. We still go out to eat sometimes, and some days we make food that is nothing close to rice and beans. However, each year we're reminded that there is room in our life to simplify and to focus more on our partners in Africa.

We hope it's clear by now that the point of the month is NOT "Eat rice and beans three meals a day for thirty-one days or you fail." Strategize and plan. Get creative. Pray about it. Do what works for your current lifestyle. Any form of participation has a significant impact. What you choose to put on your plate in March will directly impact what a vulnerable child finds on his plate for the year to come. ■

See videos from Bethany and other participants online at

EATRICEANDBEANS.COM/VIDEOS

MUCH TO LEARN

*How can our East African friends help
prepare us for Rice & Beans Month?*

by Jen Johnson

T hink about the most interesting ways you have seen food prepared, dis-
played, and served. Have you spent time with people from another culture?
Have you traveled locally or globally? Do you have friends or family
whose style of eating is different from what you're used to at home? Some of
the customs you've encountered (or the foods themselves) likely struck you
as odd, or inspiring, or both. At home in our own familiar setting, food is
as interesting or mundane as we choose to make it, but when we get the opportunity to experience the way others create meals, it can make for some
memorable eating adventures.

Early in our marriage, my husband Keith and I spent a few months in East Africa as part of a ministry internship program. We were often welcomed as guests into people's homes, usually as part of a larger gathering with other Kenyan couples in church leadership. It took some adjusting at first, but the following scenario soon felt very normal and natural:

We arrived to an exchange of warm greetings (in Swahili), often including physical contact like hugs, cheek-kissing, or, at the very least, shaking hands. As anyone new entered the room, they shook hands and exchanged greetings with every-one already there. The hosts expressed their delight at having visitors. Language and cultural barriers aside, we felt genuinely welcomed.

Prior to serving the meal, someone made their way around the table with a pitcher of water, a basin, soap, and a towel. One by one, while seated, each person washed and dried their hands. Then prayers of deep gratitude were offered, always with heart-felt thanks not only for the food, but also for the chance to share it together.

The food itself was freshly and carefully prepared. If we had arrived early enough to see a chicken wandering the premises, we probably had been looking at our dinner. Dishes like *ugali* (thick paste of white maize flour) or *chapati* (similar to a soft, thick tor-tilla) were served steaming hot from the kitchen. We knew that ingredients like rice or lentils had to be picked through for small rocks and debris prior to cooking. This meant that when those dishes were served, the preparations for our meal had started early that morning or even on the previous day. We always came away with very full bellies, and the time spent with these wise and gracious people nourished our souls as well.

Keith helps to serve a meal at a school in Kenya.

Jen helps kids with a craft project in one of the poorest areas in Nairobi.

These bountiful meals certainly were not the normal daily fare for our hosts, and were extremely rare for the people in the impoverished congregations they served. It was humbling to accept such extravagant gifts time and time again, yet we always sensed that our hosts were sincerely overjoyed to share them with us.

There was a collective reverence for the fact that many of the people from their churches would be without a meal that evening, right in the same city. We had seen firsthand how tirelessly these leaders worked to help address those needs. And they fully expected that the abundant food and fellowship we shared together would strengthen them to continue that work. Surrounded daily by hunger and suffering, they cooked, served, and enjoyed food in a way that felt truly *sacred.*

Years later, as we join with the Lahash community in Rice & Beans Month, we realize again how much our time in East Africa impacted our hearts. In some small way, we hope to recapture elements of those shared mealtimes as we reconnect with that part of the world through this month of eating simply. We're ready to slow down and proceed with gratitude. Ready to honor those with whom we share our meals, and the vulnerable whose lives we hope to impact. We know that hard days and challenges will be part of the experience, too; we expect that. Yet we look forward to moments that nourish body and soul for everyone present.

Our East African friends shared not only their food and customs with us, but they also revealed aspects of God's heart that are often lost in the fast pace of American culture. Rice & Beans Month feels like an invitation to revisit what we learned and creatively apply it to our daily life. We are both humbled and inspired to realize that even in the face of the great hunger and suffering around the world, God is inviting us into his dining room with warm greetings and much to share.

Karibuni meza. Welcome to the table. ∎

FIRST YEAR REFLECTIONS

by Casey Schilperoort

My family participated in the very first year of Rice & Beans Month. At times it felt like a bold adventure, as though we were truly standing in solidarity with the vulnerable, united against excessive consumption. At other times it just felt like we were plodding along, waiting until the month was over and wondering if our sacrifice could really make a difference.

Then it was over. And I ate a hamburger.

In April, donations started to trickle into the Lahash office in Portland. Because rice and beans make a pretty cheap meal, the money people had saved out of their grocery budgets started to add up. Eventually, 39 donations came in, and $6,400 was raised and sent to Lahash's partners in Tanzania, Uganda, and Kenya to provide food for the kids and families they support.

I remember sitting in the Lahash office on the day when we received pictures from the partnership in Tanzania. I could hardly believe what I was seeing. Giant sacks of food stacked on top of each other. Children holding bags full of beans. Mothers carrying huge sacks of flour on their heads. They had received only a third of the Rice & Beans donations, and all 75 kids in the sponsorship program received 55 pounds of maize flour and 15 pounds of beans. For many families, it would be enough food to last them for nearly a month. From 39 donations of leftover grocery money, nearly 75 families had food for a month. And that was only a third of the impact! I sat at my desk trying to soak it all in. God had multiplied our small sacrifices beyond what I could have imagined. At that moment, I knew that my family would be eating rice and beans again the following year.

The vision for Rice & Beans Month is to raise enough funds out of our leftover grocery money not only to provide immediate food distributions for hungry families, but also to lay the foundations for agricultural programs that will benefit and sustain these families for years to come. But that is only half of the picture. We want lives to be changed through Rice & Beans Month, and not only lives in East Africa. We want *your* life to be changed.

So we are inviting you to join us this March in eating rice and beans. We are inviting you to do something difficult for the benefit of people in need. We are inviting you into a month of voluntary simplicity, a month of reminding our desires and cravings that they are not in control, a month of relying on Christ to supply contentment, a month of practicing sacrificial love. A month like that could truly change your life and the lives of many others as well. ■

Families in Tanzania leave the church with sacks of flour and beans from the first Rice & Beans Month distribution.

THE HEART OF
HOSPITALITY

Learning to trade entertainment for fellowship

BY ERIN HOLCOMB

I picked up the phone and swallowed hard, not knowing how awkward this call would be. I was about to make a leap into uncharted territory. I was inviting friends over for dinner.

Hosting a meal is something I usually look forward to doing. But this time was different. It was March 2010, and it was our first venture into Rice & Beans Month with Lahash. As I held the phone, I struggled with how to combine our desire to invite guests into our home with our commitment to eating simple meals of rice and beans for the entire month.

I know I'm not the only one who has struggled with this question. From special dishes to bathroom hand towels, we are trained in our culture to offer guests only our absolute best. So how could a meal of rice and beans be sufficient to offer to the people we wanted to warmly honor? I knew I should dial and get it over with. I felt I should give our friends fair warning about what would be offered at the meal, but I was worried they wouldn't want to come. I was nervous that if they did come, they would leave our home hungry and disappointed. Really, I was afraid of being a poor host.

Hospitality is crucial to community. Christians are specifically instructed to "practice hospitality" by the apostle Paul in Romans 12, and it was even made a requirement for those being considered for leadership (I Timothy 3, Titus 1). There is something deeply spiritual and essentially human about sitting down together around food.

But I have also used hospitality to achieve much less admirable goals. I've wielded the spatula as a tool to make a good impression that will boost my ego. I've given hints to impress my guests about my social status, my good taste, my domestic skills, and my worldly palate simply by setting plates of food in front of them. I have turned a meal that should be a gift into an excuse to focus on myself, seasoned with the anxiety and self-doubt that are sure to follow such a gesture.

One of my favorite books in the whole world is the cookbook/food-theology-manifesto *More-with-Less* by Doris Janzen Longacre. In the introduction to this collection of simple food recipes, she touches on the heart of Christian hospitality in the face of our sinful pride:

> *Jesus hallowed the common meal when He broke bread, shared wine, and said, "This do in remembrance of me,"… But the word entertaining has crept into our guest-meal vocabulary. [People] used to just "have you over for dinner." Now people speak as though they are about to stage a show.*

We have forgotten that the heart of communion is the gathering of souls, not the filling of stomachs. Food gives us *a* reason to be together, but it is not *the* reason. As I wrestled with serving a plain and lusterless meal to my friends, I was really struggling with how to welcome them into my home with only my heart to offer.

I did make that phone call, and our friends did come over for a simple bowl of rice and beans. It was great. Taking the attention off the meal gave me more time and emotional energy than I usually have reserved when guests arrive. Instead of wading through courses and multiple dishes, we finished our meal relatively quickly and talked late into the evening over cups of tea. With very little to clean up, there was no rush to end our evening. And our friends loved being a part of sharing our resources with the vulnerable in East Africa. They actually appreciated being brought into our new rhythm.

I am learning to trade entertainment for fellowship. I am practicing being a warmer, more generous host by giving more of my heart and my time along with whatever food happens to fit the moment. At times that means making a very special or even elaborate meal, but these days that is rarely the better gift. I have found that opening my heart and home can be every bit as meaningful over a bowl of rice and beans. ■

RICE & BEANS
IN PERSPECTIVE

by Nina Horn

The month began with a plate of rice and beans, but for Nina Horn and her family, it certainly didn't end there.

I love that Rice & Beans Month is an invitation to consider what it's like to be in the shoes of another. That kind of awareness evokes empathy and compassion, and blurs the lines between "us and them."

We began the month with high expectations of eating rice and beans for every meal, kids included! I knew I would be making pbj's for lunch at some point, but it didn't hurt to hit the ground running. Beyond the meal plans, I thought a lot about what this experience would be like for our kids, and what I wanted it to mean to them. I want my children to do justly and love mercy (Micah 6:8); to love with passion as Jesus loves them, and to take action.

As parents, we felt the tension of wanting to stretch our children beyond their comfort zones, asking them to step outside of themselves and sacrifice some of their pleasures to help those who lack the simple necessities to sustain life. We also became aware that there was a line out there, that when crossed, changed our invitation and guidance into a requirement of rules without grace and joy. Or worse, evoked shame or guilt. So, the month was a dance of modeling sacrifice and including our children on the journey, joyfully knowing and trusting that they would willingly give as they were able.

The challenge of living in this tension became evident when we noticed that our four-

The Horns kick off the month with a plate of rice and beans.

year-old son, Jude, was still eating leftover candy from Valentine's Day at the beginning of Rice & Beans Month. We chose not to say anything about it, doubting that he would ever remember eating candy when he was "supposed to" be fasting from sugar, but feeling pretty sure he would remember if we pulled the reins on any simple pleasures. Overall, Jude maintained a joyful and celebratory spirit for the whole month. There were, however, plenty of times when both of our kids took one bite of their rice and beans at dinner and then said, "I'm done." They went to bed hungry some of those nights, and that was okay. All these parts of our family's journey helped us learn and grow.

The beauty of it all, though, was that we found ways to shift the focus from our children and spend our efforts talking about our brothers and sisters in East Africa. Talking about our differences and commonalities, pondering their lives. Opening our awareness and inviting perspective, empathy, and compassion instead of drawing battle lines over how many more bites of this or that they had to take, or whether or not they could have cake at a community dinner.

It's because of these experiences that we saw the love of God for us in new ways, and saw that same love burst forth from within our own hearts. Like when Jude emptied out his beloved treasure chest and exclaimed, "I don't need this! I want to give it to someone who doesn't have any money!" Or when he implored me to write a "sad song" with him about people who don't have homes, or money, or water. Or when we realized that maybe our family could eat rice and beans more often throughout the year and share the savings by sponsoring a child. I can see the full circle now: perspective, compassion, action, justice, relationship, transformation.

And to think it began with a simple plate of rice and beans. ■

THE CLEAN PLATE CLUB

A church's nutrition program fills more than just stomachs

BY CASEY SCHILPEROORT

Mariam and Eliyah lead the line of children as they receive lunch.

I t seems miraculous that a bowl of rice and beans can be transformed into
tangible care for a vulnerable child. That a little extra grocery money, given
with love, can show up on the other side of the world as a nutritious meal
for hungry kids. On a trip to Tanzania, I ate lunch at a small church where
this miracle happens almost every day.

BANANA

COOKED
GREENS

RICE

MEAT
STEW

I sat next to a girl named Mariam. When her mouth wasn't full of food, it was usually turned into a smile. Most of my friends don't like to have their picture taken when they're eating. Mariam didn't seem to mind a bit.

Lahash's partner, Grace & Healing Ministry of Dodoma (GHMD), provides a lunch program for children living with HIV/AIDS in Tanzania's capital city. After school, over 20 children come to the church and receive a balanced, nutritious meal. One by one, they walk through the line as the women serving them pile each plate high with rice, meat or beans, fresh cooked greens, and a ripe banana. It is more food than they would ever get at home, and quite possibly the only meal they will eat that day.

Tiffanee Wright, a former project coordinator at GHMD, has seen firsthand how the devastating effects of HIV can be compounded by hunger and malnutrition. "At the Nutrition Program," she said, "we focus on children with HIV/AIDS because we know those are the most vulnerable children in our area." She explained that studies have shown that kids living with HIV need up to 30% more calories and 50% more protein than children without the disease. "But in poverty-stricken areas where food is already a huge issue, getting that additional food is almost impossible. So children quickly lose weight, and we often see children who are severely malnourished." And while many of them are on drug therapies to manage the disease, those drugs cannot be taken on an empty stomach. Without proper meals, their health problems can quickly spiral out of control.

One of the children Tiffanee was talking about was Mariam, the little girl who ate lunch right beside me. She was born with HIV, and years of malnutrition combined with the damaging effects of her disease had severely stunted her growth. "When I first saw her," Tiffanee recalls, "she was a really cute kid, and I thought she was maybe five or six years old." But she was ten years old and barely three-and-a-half feet tall. Mariam's constant struggle with hunger and sickness had left her with the petite body of a child half her age. Her mother passed away, and Mariam was regularly left alone to fend for herself as well as to maintain the household. My heart broke for this little girl who had suffered so much at such a young age.

Mariam smiles after finishing her lunch.

But after sitting with Mariam that afternoon and watching her smile at me between mouthfuls, I could tell there was a new chapter unfolding in her story. Thanks to Rice & Beans Month, the Lahash Child Sponsorship Program, and the compassionate staff at GHMD, Mariam's life was changing one meal at a time. I thought about all the people I knew back home who spent an entire month eating simple meals.

"THIS PROGRAM IS MEETING A NEED THAT NO OTHER PROGRAM IS RESPONDING TO."

You see, the Nutrition Program at GHMD is funded directly through Rice & Beans Month donations. By simplifying their own diets, every participant plays a critical part in caring for these vulnerable kids. Tiffanee emphasizes, "We are so appreciative of people who have sacrificed in their own eating habits and included their children in eating simply, because we see the impact it has here on these children who don't have the option of choosing which foods to eat, and sometimes have no food to eat. Now we are able to fill their bellies." Because others ate rice and beans, Mariam's stomach can be filled with nutritious food that is helping to literally save her life. And her empty stomach is not the only need being filled.

"When Mariam had the opportunity to come to GHMD for the Nutrition Program, she was so excited," said Tiffanee. "It gave her an opportunity to come and be a kid. To have fun and play with jump ropes or color and talk with other kids." Now instead of rushing home after school to carry water, wash clothes, and wonder what she will eat, Mariam is able to enjoy good food and new friends.

Along with a balanced meal, Mariam and the rest of the children are discovering a new community of love and acceptance. "They not only eat together, but friendships have been developing," said Tiffanee. "Yes, they have this disease in common, but there are friendships forming that go well beyond HIV/AIDS. They support each other, they laugh together, they comfort each other. This program is meeting a need that no other program is responding to. Not only are we providing nutrition, we are providing love and support to kids who are in desperate need of those things."

I had the privilege of watching Mariam's heaping plate of food slowly become an empty plate, and I was filled with hope. Although she may never fully recover those years of lost growth, she is no longer alone. She is being loved, fed, and encouraged by a community committed to her future. A community to which you and I belong. Together, our bowls of rice and beans are being miraculously transformed into loving care for this precious girl. As you eat more simply this month, may each meal remind you of Mariam and the other children whose stomachs and hearts are being filled up because of your sacrifice. ■

FARMING FOR THE FUTURE

Kids from the Lahash sponsorship program pitch in to help clear the land in Tanzania.

The money raised through Rice & Beans Month is also helping create greater food security in vulnerable communities through sustainable agriculture programs.

In Tanzania a new plot of farmland was purchased to allow children and families to begin growing their own food. It is a training ground to teach kids and adults about farming, and the harvests will provide food for vulnerable families. "The kids will be able to learn more about agriculture and animal husbandry," said Edwin Angote, Lahash's East Africa Director. "We hope that during the rainy season they will be able to plant corn as a start."

In northern Uganda, farmland has also been purchased near Amazing Grace Children's Home. This land will help provide both food and water. Mama Susan Tabia, the founder of Amazing Grace, wrote, "The purchase of this two-acre piece of land will make it easy to identify a secure spot for drilling a well and also grow enough vegetables for food to sustain the children."

These types of sustainable food projects will continue to provide needed nutrition for a more stable and healthy future.

To find out more, visit

EATRICEANDBEANS.COM

SEEING BEYOND
BY MELINDA HAAK

We have felt many times in our marriage that we couldn't reach out to help or minister to someone because we simply couldn't afford it. We couldn't cook a meal for a friend because, frankly, we barely had the funds to feed our growing family. We didn't go out with friends for coffee because we were embarrassed to say we couldn't afford the two dollars. We couldn't support missionary friends because in most months, we were barely scraping together the money to pay rent or a house payment. Then our family joined the Rice & Beans Month challenge, excited to make a difference with the little money we had.

We learned that it is human nature to get wrapped up in our surroundings, not seeing anything beyond our own circumstances, unless we step into someone else's shoes. We have continued to participate each year, honestly, not because we can give large amounts of money, but because we want our children to enter into the lives of other kids and get a glimpse of what life is like for them. We want to expose our family to the needs of others and help them realize there are unconventional ways to help.

While this has continued to be a great experience for us, it has also brought challenges with four small children. The comments around our dinner table that month are apt to sound a bit like this:

"What gross thing are you making for dinner tonight?"

"Mommy, this is just too weird!"

"Mommy, can't we just send them money so they can get something that tastes better?"

"Open mouth. Put food in. Close mouth. Yes, you have to chew it."

Often we have to bite our tongues and pray for patience. One night after a particularly difficult dinner, a conversation was sparked by one of the videos at

Melinda's daughter scoops up another bite during Rice & Beans Month.

eatriceandbeans.com/video that features a little boy named Joseph saying "thank you" for the food that had been given him after the previous year's event. He could now eat three meals a day. My kids were a little slack-jawed when I pointed out that eating three meals a day *now* means that he was eating less than three meals a day *before.*

I'd had a complaint formally filed against me that very afternoon for having the same old snacks after school again. They wanted something new and interesting.

"Did those kids who were finally getting three meals a day get a snack option after school?" I asked. "Do you think they even had a snack after school, let alone things to pick and choose from?"

I was answered with wide eyes, shaking heads, and silence.

I don't want this month to be about shoving it down their throats. I think Joseph smiling at them from the computer and saying "thank you" with a giggle from the other side of the world is more impactful to my kids than the "eat your rice and beans because there are little children starving in Africa who would be glad to have them" speech. After seeing that video, our daughter, who was eight at the time, teared up and asked to empty out her piggy bank so that little boy could always eat three meals a day. (She also added that maybe he could buy something more than just rice and beans.)

As we continue to do this, we want to be able to send more money. More important, we want our children to see beyond themselves. We pray they will see how truly blessed they are, and that no matter their circumstances, they can always share of what they have been given. ■

CONTENTMENT BY COMPARISON

by Casey Schilperoort

E very March for the last several years, I have eaten rice and beans in some
form or another for each meal. For dinners, the whole family participates.
Typically, my wife cooks something delicious and even our son manages to
clean out his bowl.

One night I offered to cook and found myself trying to manage multiple pots
of boiling-over rice, beans that were cooking too slowly and greens that needed
chopping. In the midst of my cooking, I took a mental step back to gain a little
perspective. "This is the same meal our friends in East Africa eat every day, and
sometimes it is their only meal for the day. Sure, I'm having a hard time, but I am
cooking on an electric stovetop, not a charcoal fire. I'm grabbing spices out of a
stocked pantry and vegetables out of my refrigerator. I have no room to complain."

By comparison, I felt I should be thankful and content with what I had. Many
of the scripture verses that Lahash is focusing on this month talk about contentment. In I Timothy 6 Paul writes, "But godliness with contentment is great gain.

For we brought nothing into the world, and we can take nothing out of it. But if we have food and clothing, we will be content with that."

We have definitely struggled with being content, but not in the areas we had expected. Surprisingly, eating rice and beans all month long has not been a huge struggle. The end of the first week was definitely the hardest, and I'll admit that I am generous with the brown sugar I put on my rice and lentil porridge every morning; but for the most part, our family typically enjoys fairly simple meals throughout the year. Instead, we have noticed our discontentment creeping up in other places. Discontentment with a home that feels too small right now. Discontentment with our children as we struggle to enjoy our currently-stressful season of parenting.

Just like when I was cooking, my tendency is to grasp for contentment through comparison. It is an easy way out. How can I not be grateful for my home? In East Africa, people do so much more with so much less. Numerous people are homeless right here in my own city. How dare I struggle to enjoy my kids, while others cry out to God for the blessing of healthy children?

They are so subtle, the ways I unconsciously set myself above others, feeling content by comparison.

I can be content because at least I have more than them, right? I can tell myself it is all about gaining a little perspective on my situation. But what does this mean for those with less: the homeless, the childless, the refrigerator-less? It seems like my "perspective" allows me contentment only by denying it to them.

But what happens if I look around at my neighbors and I find out I am the one with less? Will my contentment evaporate? My contentment by comparison quickly falls flat because I am still looking at my situation instead of at my Savior. Paul has some advice: "I have learned the secret of being content in any and every situation, whether well fed or hungry, whether living in plenty or in want. I can do everything through him who gives me strength."

Then I remember.

I remember seeing joy and worship flow freely in the presence of poverty and disease in Tanzania. I remember orphaned children singing praises to their adopted Father in Uganda. I remember what it's like to worship with eyes focused heavenward rather than on what those around me do or do not have. I realize that contentment based on comparison crumbles in the face of an incomparable God, and that his presence alone brings true contentment.

And at the end of the day, our home still feels small, and parenting still is hard. But I am grateful. Not because I have more than someone else, but because I have a Savior who chose to have less. Who was rich, yet for our sakes became poor, so he could be with us in every situation.

Whether living in plenty or in want, may we all embrace this secret of being content. ∎

RICE & BEANS ANYONE?

by Virginia Whitney

In the fall of 2013, I traveled to Tanzania with the Lahash team. My experience was amazing. I would even venture to say life-changing. We stayed in people's homes, ate the local food, and rode the public transportation. While there, I had an opportunity to share a meal with some incredible kids who are part of the Nutrition Program funded by Rice & Beans Month.

A dimly-lit room in the church, which was moments before bubbling with echoes of laughter and play, became peacefully soundless as we enjoyed our meal. Each child was given a generous portion of rice, beans, cooked greens, and a banana. As we ate, I caught the occasional shy smile and curious glance from little faces around the room. One of these shy smiles was from Happy, my own sponsored child!

As we sat and shared the meal, I thought back to a potluck I had attended two years earlier with my sister's small group from her church. The whole potluck was dishes consisting of only rice and beans. Only rice and beans!?! Where are the meat and potatoes? Everyone there was choosing to eat more simply for the month of March in order to send the money they had saved on groceries to East Africa to improve nutrition for vulnerable children. At the time, the idea was so foreign to me, maybe even a little extreme. It seemed like such an inconvenience to everyday life to be restricted to a diet of rice and beans. I imagined endless explanations in the lunch room, bringing your own food to family functions, and ordering rice and beans when out with friends. I envisioned multiple socially awkward moments combined with an abundance of flatulence. Little did I know I would find myself in East Africa two years later, eating rice and beans with the kids who directly benefited from the efforts of those peculiar Portlanders.

I have two beautiful little girls of my own, and during almost every meal at home, at least one of them asks me how many bites she must take before she can be done and walk away from food untouched, wasted. I never heard that dreaded question in Tanzania. No one whined that the greens were green, or that the beans were touching the rice. The children finished their lunch with genuine appreciation for the food that had been prepared for them, something I rarely witness back home.

I work as a Physician Assistant, so after the kids had finished eating lunch, I put my professional knowledge to work and gave each of them a health check. Surprisingly, most of

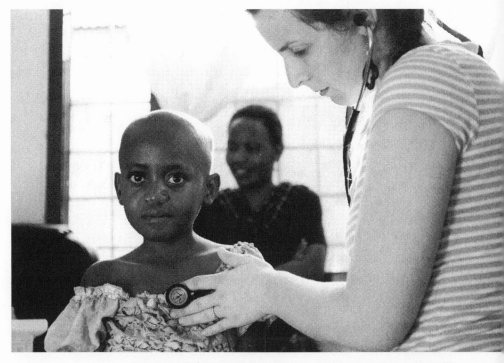

Virginia performs a health check on Happy, her sponsored child.

the children were very healthy, considering they are all HIV-positive and on antiretroviral therapy. The nutrition from these meals is vital for keeping their immune systems healthy, which reduces HIV symptoms and complications. This program has played a large role in maintaining the health of these children. The sad reality is that for many of these kids, the program provides the only meal they will eat all day.

After spending time with these kids, altering my diet for an entire month no longer seems like quite the inconvenience. Will I commit to the same level as my sister's small group did? Honestly, probably not. However, I do want to participate. During Rice & Beans Month, I plan to focus on eating more simply overall, and fitting in a few rice and beans meals throughout each week. I think baby steps are okay. Not everyone can be a peculiar Portlander, but we can all move toward this common goal of feeding a group of vulnerable children one life-changing– possibly life-saving–meal per day.

Rice and beans, anyone? ∎

FEELING FULL

One family's reflections on the highs and lows of Rice & Beans Month

BY JEN JOHNSON

Although our family initially seemed excited to begin Rice & Beans Month, it quickly became apparent that our excitement was more about the *idea* of Rice & Beans Month than the actual execution of it. During a meal-planning conversation, our seven-year-old's answer to everything was, "I don't want to eat that." Even after talking about the kids in Africa and the sacrifices that would be hard for all of us, her bottom line remained. "I don't want to eat rice and beans." Great. March hadn't even started yet.

The first week was rough. The adjustment did not go well. Some flashes of gratitude, some moments of contentment, but mostly a lot of struggles. We were hungry, and we felt *empty*. It felt like "Rice & Beans Month" was somehow expanding into "Rice & Beans For An Unpleasant Eternity."

Thankfully, God was still at work in us.

On March 7, the one-week mark, both girls were offered candy in separate situations at school. They both declined. No parental influence, just God's prompting in their hearts. They remembered and made a hard choice. When our six-year-old told my husband Keith about it, her eyes filled up with tears as she said, "I sacrificed it, Daddy."

On March 8, the recipe I tried for dinner was a flop. Morale was low all the way around the table. This Lahash devotional scripture was exactly what we needed:

> *For our light and momentary troubles are achieving for us an eternal glory that far outweighs them all. So we fix our eyes not on what is seen, but on what is unseen. For what is seen is temporary, but what is unseen is eternal.* (II Corinthians 4:17–18)

THANK YOU
FOR EATING
RICE & BEANS
LOVE WE LOVE U

The children at Kampala House in Uganda express their gratitude.

"I BELIEVE THAT GOD'S HEART IS TO SEE ALL OF HIS CHILDREN'S BASIC NEEDS MET."

We spent some time talking about why troubles are important in our lives. The seven-year-old volunteered, "If we never had anything hard happen to us, then pretty soon we would just think we are *soooo* perfect and great, and we would even think that we don't need God for anything. We would just think: *God? Who needs him?*"

The comparison of "light and momentary troubles" to eternal rewards was a turning point for us. Yet even with the positive shift at dinner that night, part of me still questioned why we were doing this *with* our kids. Eating rice and beans is much less difficult for Keith and me than for them. On many days I just wanted to say, "Never mind! Eat what you want! Enjoy your food! You're only a kid once. You can learn to have compassion for starving vulnerable children some other time. Be comfortable and happy, and for goodness' sake, have chips in your lunch again!" It would be easier in so many ways.

As I examined those thoughts, the words *comfortable, happy,* and *easy* jumped out at me. I was humbled to realize what I was doing. I was imagining ways to participate in Rice & Beans Month that would eliminate all the feelings of emptiness and struggle. Just a few adjustments, and things would be *comfortable, happy,* and *easy* in my household. I have so much to learn about what it means to follow Jesus.

Some of my best teachers are our brothers and sisters in Africa. They understand what Jesus means when he says, "Come, take up your cross, and follow me." The idea that the path into joy involves sorrows and hardship is not difficult to grasp. That is the reality of everyday life. They are not pursuing comfort and ease, but basic survival. The gospel's good news is that they do not have to be alone in those daily struggles, and that their hope will be rewarded when they reach the end.

I believe that God's heart is to see all of his children's basic needs met, so that we are free to heal, grow, and thrive in his extravagant love. I want our friends in Africa to be healthy, well-fed, educated, discipled, and ultimately to struggle *less.* To participate with God in making that a reality, I have to be willing to struggle *more.* I will have to turn away from the loud voices shouting empty promises: *"Comfortable, happy, and easy! Over here!"* I must choose to turn toward the quiet voice of Christ-in-me, inviting me into something far more real and satisfying: struggles that hold the potential to deepen and refine my faith.

Our girls could have taken the candy on March 7. We wouldn't have brought down the hammer on them for it. They're kids. It's hard. There is grace for the learning process. One sweet treat does not render Rice & Beans Month a failure. But because they chose that one small sacrifice, they experienced that "full-heart feeling" that you only get when you finally stop resisting the work God is doing in your heart and just … surrender.

When I follow the leading of Christ within, I experience the way sorrow and struggle is interwoven with joy and victory inside my heart, and within the heart of God. I get to feel his loving embrace as I look up with tears and say, "I sacrificed it, Daddy." He gets it, and I know it. I share in his ultimate sacrifice in some small way, and it does big things inside of me. That deep connection with my Savior will not make my life easier or more comfortable.

It will make my life *full.* ■

RICE & BEANS
IN COMMUNITY

by Nina Horn

Living in a new city with a new church family, Nina Horn and her family discover how community deepens the experience of Rice & Beans Month

"**M**ama, can we eat rice and beans today, pleeeaase?" my son begged as he came into the kitchen for breakfast. I wish I could say this occurred on the tenth day of Rice & Beans Month, but it was actually February 28th. I wasn't about to make rice and beans on February 28th, so I told him that we would have to wait just one more day.

Jude's enthusiasm caught me a bit off-guard. We had talked about the upcoming Rice & Beans Month and had invited our new church and other friends to join with us, but his eagerness both delighted and baffled me. When he finally got his long-awaited plate of rice and beans, he held it up with a shy smile and said, "This fills my heart with love and remembrance. Of when we used to eat together at the Lahash house."

Then I got it.

For Jude, rice and beans meant *community*. It meant being a part of something bigger, together. That's a big part of it for all of us! In part, the "something bigger" is changing our eating habits for a month and giving financially to make a difference, but it's so much more than that. It's being a part of this global community. It's being connected to our brothers and sisters in Tanzania and Uganda, and receiving the gifts of simplicity, of our hearts being moved, of a broader worldview.

There would be no meals together at the Portland Lahash house for our family. We had moved out of our Oregon home, and now "We're eating Rice & Beans in Johnstown, PA!" But we were not doing it alone. When I asked if I could make an announcement in church about the event and show a video, I had hoped for a "yes." Instead, I received an overwhelming "of course!" We opened our home for Monday night potlucks, and people came with joy. No speculation. No explanations were needed. People just wanted to know how they could participate.

I call Rice & Beans Month "a custom experience." There are so many ways to participate through simplicity, solidarity, and sharing. So when folks asked me if they could put chicken broth in the rice, I said, "Yes!" Kale in the beans? Whipped rice for dessert? Sour cream on top? Yes, yes, yes. Whether it is every meal, one meal a day, or just those Monday night potlucks, all are welcome. Come to the table; welcome to community; be a part of something bigger, together. ■

*The Horns' church community fills their home for a
rice and beans potluck.*

A CUP OF ~~COLD WATER~~ HOT UJI IN JESUS' NAME

by Casey Schilperoort

I n western Tanzania, Rice & Beans Month donations are being poured out in the form of hot porridge, called *uji* (oo-jee), into the waiting cups of vulnerable children.

During a recent visit, our new friends and partners at Path of Hope took our team out to a rural village where they have been laboring to start a new church. In a region dominated by tribal beliefs and witchcraft, this is the first church to be planted. In addition to preaching the gospel, Path of Hope has been seeking out ways to demonstrate their love by meeting the physical needs of this poor and isolated community.

In partnership with Lahash, they recently began a Sponsorship Program to provide targeted, holistic care to vulnerable children in the village. Along with school fees and medical care, they identified nutrition as a critical need. In this rural area, many families eke out a living as subsistence-level farmers or livestock herders, and their children often suffer the effects of seasonal hunger. Unfortunately, many of these children are still without sponsors to help provide the funding for their care, so the resources to meet these needs have remained limited.

In spite of these limitations, our partners clung to the truth that men (and women and children) do not live on bread alone, but on the words of God. They

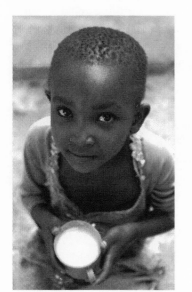

continued gathering the children together for worship and Bible lessons, all the while asking God to fill not only their spirits, but their stomachs as well.

Back in the United States, and in other parts of the world, prayers were also being lifted up on behalf of the hungry as people fasted and shared their savings during Rice & Beans Month. Thanks to these donations, all the kids at Path of Hope receive a cup of hot uji each time they gather together. Their colorful plastic cups are filled to the brim with nutritious porridge. Now when the kids come to sing and hear God's word, they leave both spiritually and physically filled. ■

145

FASTING & FEASTING

by Casey Schilperoort

I have been thinking about fasting, perhaps because we spent all of March eating rice and beans at every meal. I have also been thinking about feasting (perhaps for the same reason). I used to think of fasting only as cutting out something completely, whether it was food, coffee, or the internet. But I have been learning about another kind of fasting. The kind of fasting that simply stands against over-indulgence and embraces *less* in the presence of a continual feast.

These thoughts began to surface during a trip to Tanzania. We were staying with a Lahash co-worker who had been living in Africa for more than a year. At her home, rice and beans were the standard evening meal. One night she told us about a party she had thrown for a friend. With pride and excitement she described the meal to us: chicken curry over rice, stir-fried vegetables, fried dough with guacamole and salsa, and cake for dessert. She even showed us pictures of the meal. I distinctly remember not being able to share in her excitement. What she described to me certainly didn't sound worthy of a photograph. It just sounded like ... *dinner.*

The more I thought about this, the more I realized that what I am used to as a typical dinner (some type of meat, two or three side dishes, bread, and something sweet to finish it off) is actually a feast in most countries of the world. A feast worthy of a celebration, of gathering your friends, of remembering with a photograph. I realized that my family was indulging in a feast every day. The lavish blessing of abundant, delicious food had become a commonplace expectation. I couldn't recognize a feast even when someone showed me a picture of one.

I heard a leader from our church say, "We don't know anything about feasting if we don't know anything about fasting." From my experience, I think he was right.

Our God is a God of feasts. Throughout the Bible we see him commanding days and even weeks of feasting. Many of these feasts are instituted while his people walk through the desert. They learn about dependence and provision as they eat simple meals of manna day after day. They learn trust as their dry mouths taste water pouring from a rock. In the desert you recognize a feast when it is laid in front of you. You anticipate its coming. You appreciate its taste and the One who provided it.

But our situation is a bit different. We are not living in tents in the desert. We are not scraping sand off the manna that we gathered this morning. We have clean water pouring from stainless steel faucets instead of dirty rocks. We are surrounded by constant and seemingly endless abundance. Something changes when you live in a land flowing with milk and honey as we do. Even though it is the very place God longs to take

Casey's wife, Abbe, sorts rocks out of a basket of rice before a simple meal in Tanzania. Opposite: Casey shares a feast in a rural village.

his people, we have a tendency to forget him the fuller our bellies become.

The same thing happened to the people of Israel when God led them into the land he promised. The same people who learned trust in the wilderness quickly forgot in the presence of plenty. God recounts the sad story through his prophet Hosea:

> But I have been the LORD your God ever since you came out of Egypt. You shall acknowledge no God but me, no Savior except me. I cared for you in the wilderness, in the land of burning heat. When I fed them, they were satisfied; when they were satisfied, they became proud; then they forgot me. (Hosea 13:4–6)

God knows we have a hard time remembering him when our stomachs are constantly full. The rhythm of fasting and feasting is God's grace for us. When we step outside of this rhythm to indulge in a lifestyle of continual feasting, we tend to grow fat and proud and forgetful, enjoying the gifts over the giver. For those of us drowning in *more*, the discipline of *less* is an expression of God's love and care. God is only interested in restriction for the sake of freedom. He doesn't want to limit our enjoyment, he just wants it to be centered on him. What he wants is nearness and intimacy. He wants us to remember him.

GOD IS ONLY INTERESTED IN RESTRICTION FOR THE SAKE OF FREEDOM.

To remember that what we have is from his hand. And that whether it is a little or a lot, *it is love.* We can most properly and sincerely thank him for abundance by not greedily indulging in it at the expense of our neighbor, his creation, and our own souls.

I have been trying to figure out what all of this means for my family. Does it mean we eat more simply, so that we can truly appreciate a feast? How can our grocery store purchases show respect for our neighbor and God's creation? How can we live more responsibly and sustainably within a culture that tells us we can have whatever we want whenever we want it? How can we replace personal indulgence with sacrificial generosity?

We don't have very good answers to these questions yet, but it has been eye-opening to wrestle with them. There is a freedom that has come with realizing that our choices do not have to be ruled by advertisements and cultural norms. I am praying these lessons that God started in East Africa will continue to shape our choices and our souls. I hope we can learn to be a family that recognizes a feast when we see it. I hope that all of us can grow in gratitude and learn contentment in the rhythms of more and less. ■

*Casey's son, Asher, holds up the sign he painted for
the beginning of Rice & Beans Month.*

RECIPES

A FEW COOKING TIPS

RICE:
- Brown rice is hearty and filling. It also takes the longest to cook.
- White rice cooks much more quickly in approximately 20–35 minutes.
- Quick options such as packaged ready-to-eat rice or Minute Rice are great solutions in a pinch.
- Quinoa is a high-nutrient grain that cooks quickly (10–15 minutes) and can be used as an alternative to rice or as the base for various salads.

BEANS:
- Canned beans are generally quite high in sodium; consider low/reduced sodium versions when possible.
- Dry beans are very low cost, and not difficult to cook after you get into the rhythm of soaking beforehand. See full instructions on the next page.
- Cooking times for beans vary widely according to type. Small white beans will cook rather quickly, for example, while garbanzo beans will take much longer. Take this into consideration when cooking different varieties together in the same pot.
- Most lentils cook significantly faster than beans, taking only about 15–20 minutes, and do not require soaking in advance.
- Soaking dry beans and then discarding the soaking water before cooking is the key to reducing the gas that beans can cause.

We have a large family, so I usually double or even triple recipes. To aid in preparation, I begin soaking and cooking beans a week before Rice & Beans Month starts. I'll do 2–3 bags of beans at a time in our big stockpot, soaking one variety overnight, and cooking them next day while starting another variety soaking for that next night. After the beans have been cooked and cooled, I put them into freezer containers. Getting a head start on my "stash" really facilitates the prep process during the week.

For the rice, I use a big pot and cook a large amount at the beginning of the week, then we simply heat it up to use under or in whatever dish we are having that evening.

- Beverly Jacobson

For days when dinner leftovers are not an option for lunch, salads based on quinoa or lentils work really well. They often taste best at room temperature, so refrigerating or heating isn't a consideration. You can make a big batch on the weekend, and have it as an easy lunch or on-the-go dinner option for any point in the week.

- Jen Johnson

HOW TO COOK DRY BEANS

INGREDIENTS

1–2 pounds dried beans
2 bay leaves (optional)
¼–½ of an onion, cut into chunks (optional)
a few cloves of garlic, peeled, whole (optional)
2 tsp salt, or more to taste

DIRECTIONS

Stovetop cooking: Soak beans overnight (or 8+ hours) in a pot large enough to cover them with water by 2–3 inches. They will nearly double in volume. Before cooking, drain and rinse thoroughly. In a large stockpot or Dutch oven, add soaked beans, fresh water (covering by 2–3 inches), and bay leaves/onion chunks/garlic *(if using)*. Bring to a boil, reduce heat, gently simmer until beans are tender. This will take about 35–65 minutes depending on the type of beans. Add salt when about 15 minutes of cooking time remains. (Adding salt at the beginning will significantly increase cooking time.) To minimize foaming, you can add 1–2 tbsp of fat or oil while simmering. Add more salt to taste as desired. *(Remove bay leaves, onion chunks, and garlic cloves before eating.)*

Crockpot cooking: Soaked beans can also be cooked in a crockpot with water and seasonings as described above. It may take a little experimenting to figure out the times for various types of beans, but as a general guideline for a half-full crockpot, you can figure 6–8 hours on low, 3–5 hours on high. *(Do not overfill your crockpot or you will have a mess as the beans expand.)*

To freeze: Allow beans to cool in the pot. Strain beans, reserving liquid. Portion beans into pint or quart containers, cover with reserved liquid. (This helps preserve the beans and makes a great addition to soups or stews after thawing.) Label and freeze.

Quick-soak method: If you forget to soak beans overnight, try this method instead: In a large pot, cover dry beans with 2–3 inches of water, bring to a boil for 2 minutes, remove from heat, leave covered to soak for at least one hour. As with the overnight soak, drain and rinse thoroughly before cooking.

BLACK BEAN & TOMATO QUINOA

INGREDIENTS

2 limes, zest and juice (add more lime juice to taste)
¼ cup butter, melted and cooled
1 tbsp oil (olive, canola, or vegetable)
1–1½ tsp sugar
freshly ground pepper to taste
1½–2 cups uncooked quinoa
1–2 cans black beans, rinsed and drained (or equivalent cooked)
4–6 oz grape tomatoes, or 1 medium tomato chopped
2–4 scallions (green onions), diced
¼–½ cup fresh cilantro, chopped

DIRECTIONS

Cook quinoa in large saucepan at a ratio of 1 cup quinoa:2 cups water. Bring to a boil, reduce to a slow simmer, cook until water is completely absorbed (about 10–15 minutes), allow to cool toward room temperature. Whisk together in large bowl: lime zest, lime juice, melted butter, oil, sugar, and pepper. Add quinoa to dressing, toss until absorbed. Add remaining ingredients as well as salt, pepper, and additional lime juice to taste. Toss gently and serve at room temperature.

Submitted by Jen Johnson

BLACK BEAN BURGERS

INGREDIENTS

1 can black beans, drained and rinsed
1 cup cooked rice
¼ cup onion, finely chopped
2 tbsp salsa
1 egg, beaten
cilantro, salsa, sour cream (optional garnishes)

DIRECTIONS

Mash beans. Mix with rice, onion, egg, and salsa.
Spray skillet with cooking spray and place over medium heat.
Spoon ½ cup of mixture into skillet and flatten to ½ inch thick.
Cook 4–5 minutes on each side. Serve with optional garnishes of cilantro,
salsa, and sour cream. Serves 6.

Submitted by Bethany Campbell

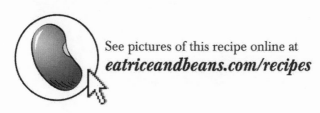

See pictures of this recipe online at
eatriceandbeans.com/recipes

BREAKFAST RICE

INGREDIENTS

½ cup cooked brown or white rice
¼ cup milk
2 tbsp honey, agave, or brown sugar (optional)
cinnamon (optional)
ground ginger (optional)
almonds (optional)
dried cranberries (optional)

DIRECTIONS

Place rice and milk in a microwaveable bowl (or heat in small pan on the stove). Sprinkle with sweeteners and spices as desired. Microwave for 1–2 minutes. Top with almonds and dried cranberries as desired.

Note: rice alone does not provide enough protein to last until lunch. Add milk, nuts, or another protein option. You can also try cooking rice with lentils for a heartier first meal.

Submitted by Bethany Campbell

BREAKFAST CROCKPOT GRAINS

INGREDIENTS

½ cup brown rice
½ cup millet
¾ cup steel cut oats
¼ cup old fashioned oats
½ cup barley

DIRECTIONS

In a large dry skillet, toast the grains over medium-low heat until they have a toasty smell. (You can skip this step if pressed for time, but it really does make it tastier.) Put grains in crockpot with 6–7 cups of water and a dash of salt. Cook on low 4 hours, or until water has been absorbed and grains are tender. Serve hot with milk, raisins, and honey or brown sugar (if using this month). Leftovers keep well in fridge to be reheated for a quick breakfast option. *Note: This "recipe" is the result of many experiments with various combinations and ratios of grains. As you do your own experimenting, notice the water-to-grain ratios and the fullness of your crockpot.*

Submitted by Jen Johnson

CHICKPEAS IN COCONUT MILK

INGREDIENTS

1½ cups cooked or canned chickpeas
2 tomatoes, diced
1 can coconut milk
4 whole cloves
4 cloves garlic, minced
1 tbsp red pepper flakes (optional)
1 tsp turmeric
½ tsp salt
cilantro for some extra flavor and garnish

DIRECTIONS

Combine all ingredients (except for cilantro) in a pot and bring to a boil. Lower heat, then let simmer for 20 minutes to let the flavors meld. Serve over brown or basmati rice. Add the fresh cilantro leaves as a garnish. Skip the red pepper flakes if you are sensitive to spicy food.

Adapted from **Extending the Table**

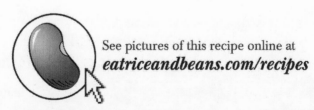

See pictures of this recipe online at
eatriceandbeans.com/recipes

COLORFUL CONFETTI BEAN SALAD

INGREDIENTS

2 cups black beans (cooked or canned and rinsed)
2 cups garbanzo beans (cooked or canned and rinsed)
2 cups red beans (cooked or canned and rinsed)
2 cups kidney beans (cooked or canned and rinsed)
1 cup fresh cilantro, minced
1 medium red onion, chopped
3 cups frozen corn
1 yellow bell pepper, chopped
4 cloves garlic, minced
1½ cups balsamic vinegar
½ cup olive oil
2 tsp sugar

DIRECTIONS

Stir the beans, cilantro, onion, corn, pepper, and garlic in a large bowl, being careful to not mash the beans. Mix the balsamic vinegar, oil, and sugar in a small separate bowl. Pour over beans and stir gently. Refrigerate the salad for at least 4 hours. Makes 15 servings. *Note: If left for one or two days in the fridge, the salad begins to burst with flavor!*

Submitted by Dan and Erin Holcomb

See pictures of this recipe online at
eatriceandbeans.com/recipes

CUBAN BEANS & RICE

INGREDIENTS

1 package saffron yellow rice
1 can diced tomatoes with green chiles
1 can corn with sweet bell peppers
1 can jalapeño black beans with lime juice

Note: If you can't find these canned combos, just add in the items separately.

DIRECTIONS

Cook saffron rice as directed on package. Combine canned ingredients in a pot and warm, stirring occasionally. Serve with the rice, and top with any of these additions: *cilantro, onion, parsley, sour cream/plain yogurt,* or *cheddar cheese (if using this month).*

Submitted by Cami Beatty

CURRIED RED LENTILS

INGREDIENTS

1½–2 sweet yellow onions, sliced
2 tbsp butter, plus ¼ tsp each of salt and black pepper
2 cups uncooked red lentils
4½ cups water
2 tbsp curry powder (or to taste)
red pepper flakes, turmeric, or cumin to taste (optional)
1 can stewed tomatoes or equivalent chopped fresh tomatoes
4–6 cloves garlic, freshly pressed
4–8 ounces fresh spinach (or substitute a package of frozen)

DIRECTIONS

If you have time, caramelize onions in butter, salt, and pepper in large skillet.
If not, sauté until tender. Add curry powder (and other spices), lentils, water,
and tomatoes to skillet (or transfer onions to a larger pot and add there).
Simmer until lentils are tender, about 15–25 minutes. In a skillet, lightly sauté
the pressed garlic (in olive oil or water) and add fresh spinach to wilt it. Add
wilted spinach/garlic mixture to the lentils. *(If using frozen spinach, just add
directly to lentil mixture.)* Serve hot over rice.

Submitted by Jen Johnson

See pictures of this recipe online at
eatriceandbeans.com/recipes

DAN'S CURRIED BEANS

INGREDIENTS

¹/₃ cup olive or vegetable oil
2 large onions, diced
10 garlic cloves, diced
1 tbsp salt
1 tbsp pepper
¹/₂–²/₃ cup curry powder
1 red bell pepper, diced
3 large tomatoes, diced
8 cups cooked or canned beans (black or other)

DIRECTIONS

Sauté onions and garlic in oil in a large pot for 15 minutes on medium heat. Add the salt, pepper, and curry powder. Cover the pot with a lid. Stir regularly. After onions and garlic have cooked down some, add the diced pepper, tomatoes, and beans. Add 1 cup of water. Simmer on medium-low for 30 minutes. Stir every 5 minutes. Remove from heat. Serve over rice.

Submitted by Dan Holcomb

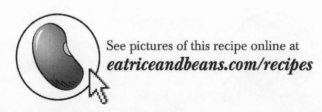

See pictures of this recipe online at
eatriceandbeans.com/recipes

DAN'S GINGER & ZUCCHINI BEANS

Note: I cook almost entirely from my head, so the directions below are estimates. It should make enough for 8–12 servings.

INGREDIENTS

3 cups dry beans or 6 cups of already-soaked beans
6 ounces tomato paste
2 diced tomatoes
1 tbsp ginger
1 tsp Italian seasoning
1 tbsp salt
1 tbsp pepper
4 tbsp butter or margarine
2 fresh zucchinis (sliced into thick rings)

DIRECTIONS

Soak 3 cups of dry black beans in water overnight. Before cooking beans the next day, rinse and drain them thoroughly.

Bring 10 cups of water to a boil, add beans to the boiling water and reduce heat to a simmer. Add other ingredients and cover with a lid. Let the ingredients simmer for 70 minutes, stirring every ten minutes.

Sample sauce to see if additional spices are needed for your taste. Serve over steaming basmati rice.

Submitted by Dan Holcomb

See pictures of this recipe online at
eatriceandbeans.com/recipes

D-I-Y RICE & BEANS

This is an easy option using whatever ingredients are on hand at the time, and each person can make it their own.

INGREDIENTS

big pot of cooked beans (pinto, white, black or a mix)
big pot of cooked rice
various toppings and sauces that your family likes

DIRECTIONS

Cook a large pot of beans according to the basic instructions on page 153.
Cook a large pot of rice.
Enlist the input of all Rice & Beans participants in the house, and have them help prepare the toppings they like best. In our family, toppings usually include some or all of the following:

diced tomatoes	*variety of red/green salsas*
plain yogurt	*diced roasted yams or sweet potatoes*
dry roasted peanuts	*any other sauces/spices someone grabs*
chopped cilantro	

Dish up bowls of basic rice and beans, and let everyone add the toppings they want that night.

Submitted by Jen Johnson

FRIED RICE

It's very important to use day-old (or older) leftover rice. Freshly-cooked rice will just make a mess. This recipe is definitely based on estimates and varies according to what we have on hand.

INGREDIENTS

2 tbsp olive or canola oil
¼–½ yellow onion, processed in food processor or finely diced
1–2 carrots, finely diced
2–3 celery stalks, finely diced
½ cup bell pepper, any color, finely diced
1 cup broccoli, finely diced
½ cup water chestnuts or jicama, finely diced
½–1 cup shelled edamame
½ cup frozen peas or fresh sugar snap peas
½–1 cup green zucchini, finely diced
3–5 eggs, or even more if you're making a large batch
2–4 tbsp sesame oil, or more to taste
2–4 tbsp soy sauce, or more to taste
4–8 cups cold day-old leftover rice

DIRECTIONS

In a large skillet (a large wok is ideal), heat oil over medium-high heat, and add chopped onion (if using). Cook until just tender, move to the sides, add carrots to the middle. (Follow this process quickly for each successive ingredient, generally adding in order from hardest to softest.) Add celery then other veggies one at a time, adding a little water as needed for steam and to prevent the pan/wok from drying out. After all veggies are added, move everything to the sides and scramble the eggs in the middle (or scramble them in a separate pan then add). Stir all eggs/veggies to combine, reduce heat to medium. Combine sesame oil and soy sauce (and processed onion, if using), stir into eggs/veggies. Finally, add the cold rice, gently stir until heated through. Adjust/season to taste with sesame oil, soy sauce, or other seasonings.

Submitted by Keith Johnson

GOOD-WITH-EVERYTHING BROWN BEANS

INGREDIENTS

3 cups uncooked pinto beans
1 tbsp cumin
1 tbsp garlic powder
3 bay leaves
½ tbsp salt

DIRECTIONS

Soak beans overnight. Rinse/drain beans and place in 3-quart crock pot. Cover with water and add spices. Cook on low for 6–8 hours or high for 3–5 hours. Enjoy as a side dish or a main dish with rice. *(Remove bay leaves before serving.)*

Submitted by India Main

HUMMUS

There are lots of hummus options in the grocery store. However, this recipe is simple, cheap, and easy to modify to suit your tastes. You can add more garlic, less lemon, water if you want it thinner, cayenne for a kick, etc.

INGREDIENTS

1 can garbanzo beans, drained (or equivalent of cooked beans)
¼ cup tahini
¼ cup olive oil
juice of one fresh lemon
1 clove garlic
½ tsp paprika
dash of tamari or soy sauce
fresh parsley (optional)
salt and pepper (or other spices) to taste

DIRECTIONS

Combine all ingredients in a food processor or blender to desired consistency.

Submitted by Jen Johnson

INDONESIAN CURRIED BEAN STEW

INGREDIENTS

1–2 tbsp olive oil
½–1 cup yellow or sweet onion, diced
1 large bell pepper, any color, chopped
2–4 cloves garlic, minced or pressed
1 can diced tomatoes
1 can kidney beans, undrained
1 can black beans, drained
1 can garbanzo beans, drained
¼ cup peanut butter
½–2 tbsp curry powder, to taste
1–3 tsp fresh ginger, minced or grated
salt and pepper to taste
¼–½ cup fresh cilantro, chopped

DIRECTIONS

Note: You can easily substitute other combinations of beans, whether cooked or canned.

Sauté onion in oil 5–8 minutes over medium heat. Add bell pepper, cook 3–4 minutes more. Add garlic, cook another minute until fragrant. Add tomatoes and kidney beans with liquid, stir. Add other beans, peanut butter, curry, and ginger, stir gently to thoroughly blend peanut butter. Reduce heat, simmer about 10 minutes. Turn off the heat, stir in cilantro and salt/pepper to taste. Serve over white or brown rice.

Submitted by Jen Johnson

LENTIL SALAD

INGREDIENTS

Lentils:
1½ cup dried lentils (1 cup dried lentils = 2 cups cooked)
2–4 cloves garlic, peeled, whole
Dressing:
3 tbsp red wine vinegar
1 tbsp balsamic vinegar
3 tsp dijon mustard
½ tbsp dried dill
¼ tsp sea salt
freshly ground black pepper to taste
4 tbsp olive oil
Salad:
2–4 green onions, finely chopped
2 large celery stalks, finely diced
2 medium carrots, finely diced
1 cucumber, finely diced
crumbled goat cheese (chevre) for garnish (optional)

DIRECTIONS

Lentils: In a large pot, cover lentils and garlic with 1–2 inches water, bring to a boil, then reduce heat to simmer. Cook uncovered until lentils are tender but not mushy (about 15 minutes). Drain lentils, discard garlic, cool lentils to room temperature. **Dressing:** In a small bowl, whisk together vinegars, mustard, dill, salt, and pepper. Slowly add oil, whisking constantly. Set aside. **Mix with salad:** In serving bowl, mix lentils with green onions, celery, carrots, and cucumber. Gently mix in dressing. Let sit for 15–60 minutes at room temperature. Garnish individual servings with goat cheese, if using.

Submitted by Jen Johnson *(adapted from The Oregonian)*

See pictures of this recipe online at
eatriceandbeans.com/recipes

LENTIL STEW WITH GREENS

INGREDIENTS

2 tbsp olive oil
1 large onion, chopped
3 cloves garlic, minced
1 tsp ground cumin
1 tsp dried cilantro
1 tsp paprika
1 tsp turmeric
1 tsp sea salt (or more to taste)
2 cups lentils, soaked and drained
2 cups chopped, packed greens
1 quart or more of chicken or vegetable stock

DIRECTIONS

Sauté onions in oil several minutes. Add garlic and spices and sauté. Add lentils and greens and cook a few minutes; add stock and bring to a boil. Simmer 30–50 minutes until tender. You can add more stock to make a thinner soup or serve over rice. Tomatoes and/or tomato sauce can be added for a different taste.

Submitted by Beverly Jacobson

LENTIL STEW WITH POTATOES

I rarely have all these veggies and spices in the house at the same time, so use whatever you have on hand, and it will be good. I do not ever use all the spices listed; they are just some that I have enjoyed in different combinations for variety.

INGREDIENTS

Main Ingredients:
2 tbsp oil
½–1 onion, chopped
2–5 (or more) garlic cloves, minced
4 celery stalks with leaves, chopped
12 cups water or vegetable stock
½–¾ cup pearl barley (optional)
2 cups dry brown lentils
4 carrots, finely chopped
3 potatoes, chopped

Spices (select to taste):
1–4 tbsp fresh ginger, minced
2 bay leaves (remove before serving)
1 tbsp paprika
2 tsp thyme
1 tsp cumin
salt and pepper

1 tsp basil
½–1 tsp turmeric
½ tsp coriander
½ tsp oregano
½ tsp rosemary

DIRECTIONS

In a large stockpot, heat the oil and lightly sauté the onion, garlic, and celery. If using barley, add the water or stock and barley next, bring to a boil, then simmer about 30 minutes as the barley takes longer to cook than the other ingredients. Add all other ingredients, bring to a boil, then reduce heat and simmer for about 20 minutes (or until lentils and potatoes are tender but not mushy).

Submitted by Jen Johnson

MEXICAN SKILLET BEANS

INGREDIENTS

2–3 cans of beans (black, pinto, red, white, kidney, or some combination) or the equivalent amount of cooked beans, drained and rinsed
1 cup frozen corn
¾–1½ cup red or green salsa
black pepper and/or chili powder to taste

DIRECTIONS

Combine all ingredients in a large skillet, cook over medium heat until simmering. Serve with rice, tortilla chips, or tortillas. Garnish with sour cream or plain yogurt, fresh cilantro, and lime juice.

Submitted by Jen Johnson

MUJADARA

INGREDIENTS

¼ cup olive oil or butter
2 large yellow or sweet onions, about 1½ lbs, sliced or chopped
1 cup brown or green lentils
½ cup basmati rice
1 tsp salt, plus more for serving if needed

DIRECTIONS

In a large (at least 12-inch) skillet, sauté onions in the olive oil or butter over medium heat. After they have softened, reduce heat a bit and stir occasionally. The key to this dish's flavor is caramelizing the onions until they are dark, rich, and toasty. This can take 30-70 minutes. While the onions are cooking, place lentils in a pot, add water to cover by an inch, and bring to a boil. Reduce heat to a simmer, cook undisturbed for 15–20 minutes until lentils are tender but not mushy. Drain and set aside. When the onions are ready, add the uncooked rice and cooked lentils to the skillet, along with 2 cups of water and the salt. Stir, bring to a boil, reduce to a slow simmer, cover, and cook. The dish is done when the rice is done and liquid is absorbed, approximately 20–40 minutes depending on size and shape of skillet. (Add more water if the liquid is absorbed before the rice is tender.) Serve with additional salt if needed.

*Adapted from **www.orangette.blogspot.com***

RICE & BEAN RAISIN COOKIES

INGREDIENTS

½ cup butter

¾ cup granulated or brown sugar

2 eggs, beaten

1 tsp vanilla

1 cup brown rice flour (or substitute black bean flour for up to ½ cup, or any other kind of flour you may have)

1½ tsp baking powder

½ tsp salt

2+ tsp cinnamon

2 cups cooked brown or white rice

½–1 cup raisins (or substitute chocolate chips or nuts)

DIRECTIONS

Cream together butter and sugar. Add eggs and vanilla and mix well. Sift together flour, baking powder, salt and cinnamon. Add to wet ingredients. Mix in rice and raisins. Drop cookie dough by teaspoons on a cookie sheet. Bake at 350° F for 12–17 minutes.

Notes: These are definitely best fresh, or eaten the same day of baking. The first time we made these, we ate them right away. The rice was a bit chewy/crispy and provided an oatmeal-like texture. The second time, I left the dough in the fridge for a day before baking, and it totally softened everything and helped the flavors mingle.

Submitted by India Main

See pictures of this recipe online at
eatriceandbeans.com/recipes

ROASTED SWEET POTATOES & BLACK BEANS

INGREDIENTS

4 medium sweet potatoes or yams (about 2½ lbs total), peeled and cubed
1 can black beans, or equivalent of cooked black beans
⅓ cup plus 2 tbsp olive oil (divided)
¾ tsp salt (divided)
2 cloves garlic, minced or pressed
1 tsp cumin
1 tsp paprika
⅛ tsp cayenne pepper
3 tbsp lemon juice
⅓ cup chopped fresh parsley
⅓ cup chopped fresh cilantro
¼ cup toasted sliced almonds for garnish (optional)

DIRECTIONS

Preheat oven to 425° F. Toss sweet potatoes with the 2 tbsp olive oil and ¼ tsp salt. Roast until tender, stirring once, about 15–25 minutes. Keep warm in large bowl. In a small bowl, combine garlic, cumin, paprika, cayenne, lemon juice, and ½ tsp salt. Whisk in the ⅓ cup olive oil and then add the parsley and cilantro. Gently combine the roasted sweet potatoes and black beans with the olive oil mixture. Garnish with almonds if desired. Serve at room temperature.

Submitted by Jen Johnson *and* Abbe Schilperoort

See pictures of this recipe online at
eatriceandbeans.com/recipes

ROASTED VEGETABLE BIRIYANI

INGREDIENTS

Vegetables:
1 large yam, peeled and cut into 1-inch chunks
1–1½ cups Brussels sprouts (if large, cut in half) or broccoli
1 red bell pepper, sliced into 1-inch strips
1 yellow bell pepper, sliced into 1-inch strips
2 large yellow onions, sliced into 1-inch slices
olive oil
1 can garbanzo beans, rinsed and drained

Garlic-Cashew Puree:
½ medium yellow onion, cut into chunks
6 large garlic cloves
2½-inch chunk of fresh ginger, peeled and cut into pieces
⅓ cup salted broken cashews
¼ cup canola oil

Rice:
2½ cups basmati rice
salt
½ tsp saffron threads, or a generous ¼ tsp of turmeric
⅓ cup milk
2 cinnamon sticks
8 green cardamom pods, lightly crushed
4 whole cloves

Garnishes:
¼ cup canola oil
3 tbsp butter
1 medium yellow onion, thinly sliced
½ cup raisins
¾ cup roasted cashews or almonds

See pictures of this recipe online at
eatriceandbeans.com/recipes

DIRECTIONS

Roast the vegetables: Preheat oven to 400° F. Combine yams and Brussels sprouts or broccoli in one large bowl, and the peppers and onions in another. Toss generously with olive oil, salt and pepper. Spread the vegetables on two large cookie sheets, leaving space between the vegetables so they have room to brown. (Do this in batches if the vegetables are crowded.) Roast for 15–20 minutes, until they begin to soften and color.

Make the garlic-cashew puree: While the vegetables are roasting, combine all puree ingredients, except the canola oil, in a food processor and puree. Pour in the oil and process until completely combined.

Remove the vegetables from the oven and divide the garlic-cashew puree equally between the pans and toss the puree gently but thoroughly with the vegetables. Return pans to the oven and roast another 10–15 minutes until the vegetables are nicely browned. Scrape all roasted vegetables into a large bowl. Stir in garbanzo beans. *Note: The vegetables can be made a day ahead and kept covered in the refrigerator.*

Make the rice: Rinse the rice, then soak in water for 30 minutes to 6 hours. Drain. Fill a 6-quart pot ²⁄₃ full of water. Add 3 tbsp of salt and bring to a boil. Add rice and cook it like pasta, about 5 minutes, or until tender but with a slight firmness. Drain immediately and spread the rice on a cookie sheet so it cools quickly. Lightly toast saffron or turmeric for 30 seconds to 1 minute in a small, dry saucepan over medium heat. Immediately add milk. Remove pan from heat and set aside to steep for a minimum of 20 minutes.

Assemble the biriyani: Preheat the oven to 325° F. Butter the inside of a 9x13-inch baking dish. Mound the vegetables in the center and cover with rice, patting it into a smooth dome. Tuck the cinnamon sticks, cardamom pods and cloves into the rice, and drizzle the entire dome with the saffron (or turmeric) milk. Tent foil over the dome so it does not touch the rice. Seal it around the edges of the dish, then bake for 45 minutes to 1 hour, or until hot at the center.

Make the garnishes: Meanwhile, prepare several layers of paper towels on a plate. In a 10-inch skillet over medium-high heat, warm the oil and butter and fry the onions until crisp. Lift out with a slotted spoon, spread on the paper towels and sprinkle with salt. Fry the raisins until they puff, and scoop them out onto the towels. Finally, briefly fry the nuts until golden.

Remove the biriyani from the oven and lift off the foil. Remove the whole spices. Scatter the garnishes over the top of each serving.

*Adapted from **splendidtable.org***

ROD'S THAI-SPICED KALE & BEANS

INGREDIENTS

2 cups uncooked kidney beans
2 tbsp olive oil
1 large onion, diced
2 tbsp garlic, minced
1 cup green and red bell peppers, finely chopped
2 cups kale or other greens, finely chopped
1–2 cups sliced mushrooms (optional)
½–1 cup red or green Trader Joe's Thai curry sauce
salt

DIRECTIONS

Soak kidney beans overnight, thoroughly rinse and drain. Put beans in slow cooker and cover with 1–2 inches of water. Add all ingredients except mushrooms and curry sauce, cook 3–6 hours in slow cooker until beans are tender. Sauté mushrooms in olive oil until *lightly* cooked, add to pot. Add Trader Joe's Thai Curry sauce and salt to taste. Stir to combine, serve over rice.

Submitted by Rod Willett

See pictures of this recipe online at
eatriceandbeans.com/recipes

SPICY BLACK BEANS

This recipe fills a large stockpot, so you'll have enough to serve a group, or have leftovers, or freeze for future meals.

INGREDIENTS

4 cups uncooked black beans
10–14 large cloves garlic, pressed
1½ tbsp soy sauce
2 tsp black pepper
2 tsp sugar
1–2 tsp ground ginger
2 tsp salt
1½ tsp sesame oil
1–2 tsp ground cumin
½–2 cups diced onion
1 tsp–1 tbsp dried red pepper flakes (1 tsp is "kid-friendly")

DIRECTIONS

Soak beans overnight in water. Drain and rinse beans thoroughly, and cover with 2 inches fresh water in large stockpot. Add remaining ingredients. Bring to a boil, reduce heat and simmer partially covered until beans are tender, about 2 hours, stirring occasionally. Add more hot water if necessary to keep beans from drying out or to reach a thinner consistency.

Serve over rice. Garnish with dry roasted peanuts, fresh cilantro, red or green salsa, sour cream, or plain yogurt.

Submitted by Jen Johnson

SWEET POTATOES WITH BLACK BEANS & RICE

INGREDIENTS

1 cup white rice
2 cups cooked black beans, or 1 can drained and rinsed
2 sweet potatoes, peeled and chopped into ½-inch cubes
½ cup fresh cilantro, chopped
juice of 1 lime
1 jalapeño pepper, minced (optional)
salt and pepper
sour cream or plain yogurt

DIRECTIONS

Preheat oven to 400° F.

Bring two cups water to a boil. Add rice and ½ tsp salt. Cook until water is absorbed, 15–20 minutes. Add black beans and keep warm.

Place sweet potatoes on a baking sheet with a drizzle of olive oil, salt, and pepper. Roast in the oven until tender and just starting to brown, about 25 minutes. Combine beans and rice with chopped cilantro, lime juice, jalapeño, and sweet potatoes. Season with salt and pepper to taste. Garnish with sour cream and more cilantro. *Note: Makes a great filling for tortillas.*

Submitted by Bethany Campbell

TEXAS CHILI

INGREDIENTS

1 onion, diced
3–5 cloves garlic, minced
1 tbsp chili powder
1 tbsp cumin
2 cans diced tomatoes (I use fire-roasted tomatoes)
1 tbsp cornmeal flour
1½ tsp salt
1 tbsp dried oregano
1 can kidney beans
1 can black beans
1 can pinto beans
1–2 cans of water (depending how thick and chunky you like it)
½ cup leftover coffee (optional, but it's the secret ingredient)

DIRECTIONS

Heat enough olive oil to thinly coat the bottom of a large Dutch oven. Sauté onion until just tender, add garlic to pot and sauté one minute. Add the next two spices, sauté one minute. Add tomatoes to pot, and and then add remaining ingredients, varying the amount of water you add based upon how thick you like your chili. Allow chili to heat through and slowly simmer for 15 minutes. Season to taste with salt or other seasonings. Serve hot, topped with cheese, sour cream, and a large handful of crumbled corn chips (depending on how decadent you are allowing yourself to feel this month).

If you are cooking with dried beans rather than canned, which works equally well, allow 1 cup of each type of bean to soak for 5–6 hours. Rinse and drain beans. After you have sautéed your onion, garlic, chili powder and cumin, add beans back to the pot containing the remainder of ingredients. Bring to a boil, and then reduce heat to a gentle simmer for 45–60 minutes, or until tender. Watch beans as they cook, making sure to gradually add water if the beans become uncovered. Season to taste and top with desired toppings.

Submitted by Abbe Schilperoort

WHITE BEAN SOUP

INGREDIENTS

2 tsp olive oil
1 large onion, chopped
2 cloves garlic, minced
3–4 cups cooked white beans (we use navy beans)
about 2 quarts chicken or vegetable broth
2 bay leaves
2 tsp cumin
½ cup uncooked rice
2 cups chopped, packed greens
salt and pepper to taste

DIRECTIONS

In large stockpot, heat oil and sauté onions until tender. Add garlic and sauté. Add beans, broth, bay leaves, and cumin. Bring to a boil, reduce heat and add rice (can also use couscous). Cover and simmer until rice is done. Add greens, salt and pepper to taste, and cook a few more minutes until greens are wilted.

Submitted by Beverly Jacobson

APPENDIX

Download all of the following resources and more at

EATRICEANDBEANS.COM

TIPS FOR **EVERYONE**

The following tips are designed to help you prepare for Rice & Beans Month, and then stay engaged in meaningful ways. Use the ideas that seem helpful to you; skip the ones that don't!

- **Try a practice meal before Day One.** Find a couple of recipes or meal ideas that sound doable, and try a "practice run" here and there to give you an idea of what it will be like to prepare and eat different foods.
- **Check the fridge.** As Day One approaches, think about what you want to find in your fridge and cupboards. For example, if you have meat lasagna for dinner the night before you begin, chances are there will be leftovers in the fridge the next day. Eating a pile of pasta, beef, and cheese on the first day of Rice & Beans Month might not help you focus on *simplicity, solidarity, and sharing.*
- **View videos and other media.** Lahash has some beautiful videos and blog posts at *lahash.org* and at *eatriceandbeans.com.*
- **Research the region.** Learn a bit about East Africa to be better informed about the issues this part of the world is facing.
- **Estimate your food spending.** If you do not know how much you usually spend on groceries and restaurant meals in a month, take note. It will help you keep track of how much you are saving by switching to a modified diet.
- **Cook some dry beans.** Even if you've never used dry beans before, it is easy to learn how. (find basic instructions on page 153) After they have been cooked and cooled, they freeze well and come in handy for putting a meal together quickly.
- **Add a small appliance.** Neither a crockpot nor rice cooker is essential, but if you can get a good deal on one or both of them secondhand, you will be glad you did.
- **Eat in community.** Whether you open your home or show up at a potluck, make every effort to eat with other participants when you can. Definitely figure out the best ways to share recipes with each other!
- **Cook in quantity.** Cooking larger quantities of rice and beans doesn't take a whole lot more effort than cooking small quantities, and leftovers can be a helpful solution for lunches or meals-on-the-go.

Please don't hesitate to share other ideas or practices that make Rice & Beans Month more doable for you. Send an email to *info@eatriceandbeans.com*, or post at *Facebook.com/EatRiceAndBeans!*

TIPS FOR FAMILIES WITH KIDS

Although there are challenges, participating in Rice & Beans Month with children is a wonderful way to expose them to the concepts of *simplicity, solidarity, and sharing* right at their level of understanding. Lots of families have made it work with various modifications and tons of grace. Here are some of our best ideas and recommendations:

Engaging With Your Kids
- **Start slowly.** Think of your family's first year as a foundation to build on in future years. Focus on the themes and the more kid-accessible materials like videos, photos, and the "For Kids" sections in the daily devotions of *A Common Meal*. Experiment with dietary changes rather than enforcing them.
- **Keep talking.** Through praying together and through regular family conversation, help kids grasp the vision and purpose of the month and expand their awareness of the needs of others.
- **Be confident and positive.** Don't assume it will be easy, but don't assume it will be torture, either. Come to terms with the likely possibility of your kids experiencing hunger, voicing complaints, or struggling at times. Kids will survive. Parents will survive. Everyone will learn and grow. You will likely have many times of being pleasantly surprised at how well it goes or how deeply the concepts sink into your kids' hearts.
- **Involve the kids.** The more they feel a part of it, the more they will embrace it. Little ones can help scoop food onto plates, decorate money-collecting jars, or click "play" on a video. Bigger kids can be involved in meal planning and preparation, reading the devotions aloud, or even choosing their own unique foods to give up.
- **Empower kids to speak out.** The concrete nature of the event makes it easy for kids to explain in their own words. The more they talk about it with grandparents, neighbors, or friends, the more they will take ownership of it for themselves. Kids have been some of our very best advocates for the event! You'll also get to hear them say some funny, poignant, and surprising things.

Practical Considerations

- **Find a special sauce.** Identify a handful of condiments or sides that just seem to make everything taste better. Whether it's sour cream, soy sauce, tortillas, a certain type of seasoning, or whatever, use it liberally. If different kids each have a different "special sauce," make sure they're all available on the table!
- **Utilize go-to recipes.** Most families have these anyway, the dinners that come together easily and everyone enjoys. Figure out your "Rice & Beans Go-To Recipe," and keep the ingredients on hand.
- **Take breaks.** If your family is eating rice and beans a lot of the time, make sure the kids know when the breaks are coming. It might be a family birthday party or a built-in weekly celebration meal, or even a simple meal that is still cheap but isn't rice and beans (like breakfast-for-dinner).
- **Use the resources.** The videos and photos posted at *lahash.org* and *eatriceandbeans.com* are great ways to engage kids. There are many short articles in the Stories section of ***A Common Meal*** as well as a section of each daily devotion that is designed just for kids.
- **Prep for mealtime activities.** Have a supply basket for the kitchen table so you're ready for all of the activities presented in the kids' devotions. Include paper, pencils, crayons, and a tablet or other device for easy access to the videos that are referenced. Some families have used money jars to involve kids in tangibly adding to the savings as the month progresses.

And don't forget **Parent Solidarity!** Let us know if you find some of these suggestions helpful, and please share other ideas that make Rice & Beans Month more doable for you and your kids. Send us an email at *info@eatriceandbeans.com,* or post at *Facebook.com/EatRiceAndBeans!*

GUIDE FOR **GROUPS OR CHURCHES**

Rice and beans definitely taste best when eaten in community! Use the following basic outlines to help structure your group gathering times. All of the outlines can certainly be tailored to fit your specific group.

Plan unique events for your Kick-Off Dinner and Celebration Feast.

OPENING EVENT: Rice & Beans Kick-Off Dinner

- Schedule it 1–2 weeks prior to March 1 or Ash Wednesday
- Serve a lunch or dinner of various of rice and beans dishes, either potluck-style or have a few designated volunteers cook specific recipes in quantity
- Consider including recipe cards for the dishes served
- Provide printed copies of the Introduction to Rice & Beans Month (download at *eatriceandbeans.com*), have copies of *A Common Meal* available (or direct folks to order online)
- Include a brief program. Show a video from *eatriceandbeans.com/video*, have a couple of previous participants share about the impact of their experiences, or have some Q&A time as you enjoy the meal!

CLOSING EVENT: Celebration Feast

- Lunch or dinner gathering after March 31 or Easter
- Potluck style, encourage participants to contribute some favorite foods that they missed during Rice & Beans Month (no rice or beans allowed!)
- Provide an opportunity to gather donations of saved money (or direct folks to give online)
- Facilitate a time of sharing about the struggles, joys, insights, or inspiration
- Prayers of gratitude and prayers for the donations to make a great impact in East Africa!

WEEKLY GATHERINGS:

Partake: enjoy a potluck meal of rice and beans

Ponder: brief program to facilitate group interaction
- **Open Forum** – invite participants to share any insights or personal impact
- **Reflection Time** – *For each gathering, choose one of the following pairings of devotions and videos. All are well-suited for use with groups. The videos can be found online at **eatriceandbeans.com/video**. If children are part of your gathering, prepare in advance to include them in the "For Kids" reading and activity*
  - Devotion – **Day 2**
  - Video – **"Wisdom from Mama Esther"**

  - Devotion – **Day 22**
  - Video – **"Welcome to Rice & Beans Month"**

  - Devotion – **Day 18**
  - Video – **"Cooking with Kabang"**

  - Devotion – **Day 28**
  - Video – **"My Rice & Beans Experience"**

  - Devotion – **Day 27**
  - Video – **"Thank You from the Kids"**

  - Devotion – **Day 7**
  - Video – **"Thank You from Joseph"**

  - Devotion – **Day 37**
  - Video – **"Sauda's Story"**

Pray: focus on our East African brothers and sisters and the participants at the gathering

ABOUT **LAHASH INTERNATIONAL**

Lahash International partners with local ministries across East Africa to bring good news and holistic care to children in need. At the grassroots level, we confront the effects of HIV/AIDS, wars, refugee crises, and extreme poverty. Kids who at one time were without hope are now thriving under the loving care of many from around the world who have joined this joyful endeavor.

For more information on Lahash International,
visit *lahash.org*.

NOTES

NOTES

NOTES

Made in the USA
Charleston, SC
19 January 2015